Beginners' Guide to Writing & Selling Quality Features

A Simple Course in Freelancing for Newspapers/Magazines

Charlotte Digregorio

Civetta Press
P.O. Box 1043
Portland, Oregon 97207-1043

D1010005

Published by: Civetta Press
P.O. Box 1043
Portland, Oregon 97207-1043
(503) 228-6649

First printing 1990

Library of Congress Catalog Card Number: 89-91823

ISBN: 0-9623318-0-5

_____

Printed and bound in the United States of America

Dedication

This book is dedicated to my students who encouraged me to write it, and also to the published feature writers to-be who will read it. To all of you, many years of pleasure, personal fulfillment, recognition, and success! And, to many of you, let this be the start of a rewarding home-based career!

Charlotte Digregorio

Acknowledgments

Special acknowledgment and thanks are given to the following publishing companies for generously granting permission to reprint material in this book.

- "If 'Cold Calls' Freeze Brokers' Spirit, They Can Warm to the Job," By John Andrew. Reprinted by permission of *The Wall Street Journal*, Copyright Dow Jones & Company, Inc., 1984. All Rights Reserved Worldwide.

- "Can-Do Classic in Midwestern Town," By Andrew H. Malcolm. Copyright 1987 by The New York Times Company. Reprinted by permission.

- "Slow Descent into Hell," By Jon D. Hull. Copyright 1987 Time Inc. Reprinted by permission.

- Christopher W. French, *The Associated Press Stylebook and Libel Manual*, Copyright 1987 by The Associated Press. Reprinted by permission of Addison-Wesley Publishing Co., Inc., Reading, Massachusetts.

- "Miniature Horses Still Like To Think Big," By Teresa A. Moss, Nov. 27, 1988. Reprinted from *The Bulletin,* Bend, Oregon.

(Acknowledgment also given on page where material is reprinted).

Preface

You can't write features and get published, you say?

I say you can, no matter who you are!

I'll make this preface short and sweet because I'm anxious for you to start right in with Chapter One.

This book makes writing and getting published easy by giving you basic details you won't find in other books. That's a promise from a journalist and trained educator.

For simplicity, throughout this book I've used the pronoun "he" most of the time, rather than take up space writing "he or she." (Often, I've found it difficult to substitute "they" to avoid use of those singular pronouns.) I hope you don't find the often used "he" offensive.

Charlotte Digregorio

Table of Contents

Chapter V
Writing the Feature 49

Chapter VI
Be Your Own Editor 81

Chapter VII
Finishing Touches 109

Chapter VIII
Getting Published 123

Appendix 145

Index 149

I

Let's Get Acquainted

Writing features—including those about people, the arts, lifestyles, travel, how-to and seasonal articles—is easy to learn and enjoyable. And, seeing your name on a published article is a thrill!

This book is intended for those who aspire to writing features for newspapers and magazines, but don't know how to begin. It is also very helpful for public relations professionals who write features for promotional purposes, staff journalists without feature experience, and students writing for school publications.

Writing and getting published isn't difficult if you know journalism basics. This is a practical and frank guide, "workbook and tutorial," with a common sense approach which instructs through painless examples and exercises. But no textbook learning here—just a clearinghouse of information, cut, dried, and chewed. This book not only emphasizes step-by-step basics of writing and marketing articles, but it covers the needed legwork before writing begins, such as finding article ideas.

For the most part, books written about freelancing are unrealistic. They assume you know journalism basics, and they don't focus exclusively on features. Many of these books are written by freelancers who have never worked on a journalism staff, so essential points are omitted. This book will train you to think like a working journalist on a staff publication.

As for marketing articles, other books assume you can reach the big time publications without taking the steps of starting with the small ones and working up to the large ones. This book outlines basic methods and makes no false assumptions.

Ever wondered about:

• How to regularly locate simple, but interesting and marketable feature ideas?

• How to prepare for an interview? How many questions to ask? Which questions are appropriate and which aren't? What methods to use to gather and record facts accurately without taping? How to encourage a poor communicator to be specific and avoid digression? Journalistic ethics? How long an interview should last?

• Journalistic style? How to begin an article with a bang and maintain the reader's attention? How to organize interview information into paragraphs with logical sequence and smooth transitions? How short paragraphs should be?

- How to write snappy, concise sentences with bright words?

- When and where to use direct quotes, and to what extent they can be altered?

- What abbreviations are acceptable in a journalistic article?

- Whether to let an interviewee read your article before submission?

- How to submit a professional-looking article with proper heading and page identification?

- How to market articles? What publications and which editors to approach first? What tactics to use to ensure your submission will be run? What steps to use to target and get published in mid-size and large publications (both general interest and specialty) which offer great pay and exposure? How to mail articles with proper cover notes?

- What common journalistic terms mean? "Stringer," for example? (If you know some basic journalistic lingo, which is simpler to grasp than legalese, you'll be able to communicate well with editors.)

Well, "stringer" (freelancer), you'll learn answers to these and hundreds of other frequently-asked questions. This book is filled with vital information, including warnings of common beginners' mistakes, and I hope you'll find it to be personal, lively, and concise.

By learning this book's basics, you'll avoid years of trial and error, submission rejection, and discouragement. For the most part, editors don't have time to rewrite features even if the article idea is excellent or unusual.

In reading this book, you'll forget the English composition style of your junior high and high school years, that which editors trash. Journalism is different, with its own language and form, but easy to grasp.

I know, because I started from scratch. In this book, I include my experiences—those of a self-made, practicing and teaching journalist who entered the field without ever having taken a journalism course. I began at an entry-level staff job, after having been a foreign language teacher. My journalism career has included positions as a newspaper feature editor and magazine editor, and currently, I'm a freelance writer and university journalism instructor.

I also include anecdotes of my students, from homemakers with high school diplomas, to college students and working professionals with graduate degrees, who've gotten published as a hobby, sideline, or who've even made a career out of it.

Whatever your background, you can be a great feature writer. No, you don't have to be creative, but if you learn these skills, your readers will think you are! So, writing features is simply a skill to be learned, just like plumbing or carpentry. Journalists aren't creative people per se, but technicians who gather and arrange facts in a colorful way.

And as a freelancer, you can learn to do better, more careful work than a staffer who works under constant deadline pressure. Look through any publication and you'll notice some bad writing.

This book includes these simple examples and exercises: analysis of good and bad features; a hypothetical interview; reconstruction of an article with jumbled paragraphs; and practice in writing tight sentences. No need to take an evening seminar to learn basic feature writing skills!

Use this as a workbook: underline the text and take notes in margins for maximum assimilation.

I've written this book because there's increasing need for freelance submissions as journalism staffs narrow in the 1990's due to budget cutbacks. And features—unlike news articles with complex fact gathering which could result in libel—are easy for a competent beginner to sell.

Finally, writing features is fun because you learn about interesting subjects and people. Ever wondered about what it's like to be a skydiver?...Start by interviewing one. You'll have the privilege of entering into another's life. (And, it's fun to chat with people.)

New horizons ahead! Sharpen your pencil!

II

What Is a Feature?

What is a feature "story?" First, realize that when journalists use the word "story," they don't mean fiction, but an article.

A feature story is most commonly found in a newspaper's Living section or in its Sunday magazine supplement, for example. It's a story with an element of human interest—one which appeals to your emotions. It involves subjective observation, as it's seen through the writer's eyes. And, it's descriptive with picturesque adjectives and verbs, and has casual language and style.

You probably read many news stories, but unlike features, they are straightforward with only the facts and no subjective observation. In news stories, adjectives, which create subjectivity, are avoided.

Let's discuss the feature's subjective style. If the story is about a person, then besides telling facts about who the person is and what he does, you're describing characteristics about him as you observe them. If, for example, you make a statement like, "He looked much younger than his 20 years," that's subjective. To you, he may look that way, but to me, he might look his age. But as a feature writer, you are entitled to your perspective. Hopefully, it would be much like the readers' opinion, had they seen him.

Even though the story includes subjective observation, unless you are writing a first person feature, such as a travel experience story, you usually wouldn't use the pronoun "I" in telling the story. If you absolutely must make reference to yourself in the non-first person story, then refer to yourself as "this writer."

As for other elements, features must be interesting and/or entertaining, contain direct quotes from interviewees, and be timely and relevant to the publication they appear in.

Use your common sense. You wouldn't expect to see an article about someone who toboggans, appearing in a publication during summer. And, you wouldn't see a story about a person who lives in California, appearing in a small-town Arizona newspaper, unless there was something in that person's life which would link him to that town.

Topics of Features

Let's consider common kinds of features which are popular with editors. Some of these categories are broad and may overlap.

1. *People*—These stories are among the most common and popular.

   - *Someone with an Interesting Hobby, Job, or Business.* For example, an antique car collector, a dollhouse builder, a costume designer, a mannequin restorer.

   - *Someone Well-known who is Retiring or Moving Away.* For example, a person who has been active in community affairs, such as one who has volunteered much time to helping the underprivileged.

   - *A Unique Child.* A computer whiz or a track and field star, for example.

   - *A Unique Senior Citizen.* For example, someone who's earning money during retirement in an unusual way. (I once read about a senior who became a full-time magician, performing at parties, after he retired from sales work.)

- *A Unique Handicapped Person.* One who is very independent. (I once wrote a feature about a blind woman who cooked for 12-person home dinner parties, sewed her own clothes, and square-danced, among various activities. I spent a day observing her and wrote about her maneuvers.)

- *Artists.* Try some of the more unusual ones such as a blacksmith, a glassblower, a mime, barbershop singers, an ethnic music band. (One of my students wrote about a guitarist who earned a full-time living by playing on a street corner.)

- *Famous Person who Comes to Town.* You've often read about a famous person who's visiting, and besides his professional life, you learn about his private life: his likes, dislikes, beliefs, and hobbies. (It seems staff journalists hoard these stories, but if you have contacts and know of someone connected to the celebrity, you can persuade an editor to let you cover the story.)

2)   *Events*

- *Public Gatherings.* For example, annual festivals, exhibits, concerts, shows. This type of feature would include a summary of information about participating performers and activities offered (ones that are most interesting), along with direct quotes from some performers and a few spectators. (When I lived in a rural area, I wrote stories about the annual corn and pumpkin festivals.)

- *Uncommon Happenings.* For example, the birth of a second set of twins to a mother, or the marriage of one set of twin sisters to a set of twin brothers in another family.

3) *Lifestyle*

- Features about, for example, what it's like being a single parent raising a family, what it's like to live in mobile homes or house-boats, or what it's like being a teen-ager these days. These features involve inter-viewing more than just one person to obtain a sampling of different viewpoints. (In recent years, a lot of lifestyle features have been beaten into the ground, but you can find new angles.)

4) *Seasonal*

- *Observance of Holidays.* For example, how a particular ethnic group celebrates Christmas.

- *Fashion.* What's coming back in? You often read about how a particular accessory is back in style. These features include comments and direct quotes from fashion experts or salespeople and the public.

- *Food.* For example, a seasonal dish, popular abroad, which is becoming a favorite here.

- *Sports.* One that's becoming a fad.

5) *Trends of the Decade*

Features about, for example, women and men entering fields which were traditionally limited to a certain gender, or new types of businesses becoming popular. With the latter, in the 1980's, we read features about sun tan salons and tatoo businesses. In this category, a feature would involve interviews with more than one person.

6) *Anachronisms*

For example, features about businesses which are becoming extinct such as soda fountain shops. This type of feature would include an interview with the business owner for his perspectives on what it used to be like, compared to now—how its patrons have changed since the old days, etc.

7) *Interesting Places to Visit/Travel to*

For example, local, regional towns or institutions, or more general features, such as those about foreign countries which are becoming popular to Americans (or those which have yet to be discovered by us). These features are written in the first person, because personal opinion is essential in them. They also contain direct quotes from others such as travel companions or people met along the way such as innkeepers. (I once wrote a feature about a turkey farm, and have written others about interesting museums. I'd included direct quotes from those working at these places.)

8) *Informational*

Features about, for example, services offered to the public by the government or by social service agencies. (One of my students wrote a feature about the federal government's Small Business Administration program to help those starting businesses. Some of my other students have written about programs to combat drug and gambling problems. The latter features included interviews with former addicts and how the program helped them. Extensive details were included on the program itself with the writer's observation on particular activity there, quotes from the program's director, and comments from program counselors on the particular addiction.) Features on social problems usually involve much more fact gathering and work than other features, and they turn into a long magazine story or a series of stories in a newspaper.

9) *How-to*

These cover a range of topics including: self-help, such as improving your health, staying fit, and emotional well-being; home improvements and car mechanics in men's specialty publications; and interior decorating in women's publications. How-to stories involve interviewing a couple of experts on the topic and quoting them on their ideas and opinions, along with interviewing people who've benefitted from their advice. (I've written simple how-to stories on making maple syrup, holding garage sales, and practical ways of earning money in your spare time, by interviewing people actively involved in these activities.)

10) *First Person Experience (Non-travel)*

For example, the most effective ones are those where the writer has participated in some different or unusual activity, and shared his perspectives. (Instead of writing about a farmer's way of life, I once visited a farm and became a farmer for a day, describing experiences firsthand in my feature.) These first person features include direct quotes from others involved. You will most commonly run across these features in the Sunday magazine supplements of newspapers.

How to be a Good Feature Writer

A good feature writer works at acquiring observation and concentration skills. If you're writing about a person, for example, focus on being alert when you're talking to him. Notice his demeanor, his movements, and how he speaks (his tone, for example). If you're writing about someone with an interesting hobby or job, it's important to gain an appreciation of his methods and expertise.

If you interview a person with an interesting hobby, ask him to demonstrate as much as he can on how he does it, and observe him during a typical day. If you interview a violinmaker, for example, concentrate on how his fingers move with dexterity as he strings the instrument.

Have you ever noticed how a doctor sews stitches? He works with the ease of a tailor sewing a button. When I interviewed a doctor in a hospital's emergency room, I observed this and made this analogy in my story to give readers a clear image.

Ever noticed how a policeman walks? When I interviewed a policeman for a story, I noticed that he walked with his elbow slightly outward, even before he put on his holster, because he was used to carrying a gun around his waist. I also noticed that every time he emerged from his patrol car, he scanned his surroundings to prepare for possible danger.

I had a student who wrote a feature about a strolling violinist at a restaurant. She not only included observation on how and what the violinist played, but she was also alert to the interesting reactions he got from the patrons.

Another way of becoming a good feature writer is to regularly read many articles, particularly those of famous journalists, even those who aren't features writers. Columnists, for example, are a good choice because they write with much feeling and personality. Read syndicated columnists such as Mike Royko or Bob Greene, because they are observant and entertaining.

Among publications which consistently run good, well-developed features are: *The New York Times,* the *Los Angeles Times,* and *The Wall Street Journal.*

Stay away from publications which lean toward gossip-oriented features on celebrities, and those which run short, quick-reading features which are lacking in content. I refer, without naming specific ones, to those which are commonly found at supermarket check stands.

Whenever you see local publications, such as neighborhood and community papers, pick them up. Get a feel for what kinds of features are being written locally, particularly if you plan on submitting stories to local publications.

Anyone can write good features. From the beginning, it's easy and enjoyable, and your goal will be to improve a little with each new story. Most features you read, even in major publications, aren't very well written. After you finish reading them, you find that basic questions about the topic remain unanswered. You can do better yourself!

I love to write features, particularly those about people who have interesting jobs. I've always wondered what it would have been like, had I pursued a different line, and through my writing, I find out.

Analyzing Features

In reading features, I don't believe in analyzing them to the point of tearing them apart, because then, you will lose the enjoyment of reading. But, in the beginning, we'll be looking closely at features and picking out their main good and bad elements.

The following story, "Miniature Horses Still Like To Think Big," by Teresa A. Moss, is reprinted from *The Bulletin* in Bend, Oregon. It is an interesting and well-written story. As you read it, think about why it qualifies as a feature. Before you read the commentary, number the story's paragraphs (all indentations, even those with just direct quotes), so you can readily follow it.

They look like horses, smell like horses and neigh like horses. Yet they ride in the family station wagon and step into the house to watch television.

Occasionally they are invited to curl up on the living room sofa or settle into their owner's lap to drift off to sleep.

"I've got pictures of a guy with one on his bed," said Jean Kenneth, who recently opened Mountain High Miniatures, the first miniature-horse ranch in Central Oregon.

Kenneth, 55, breeds, sells and shows the small horses, which can be as short as 26 inches at maturity.

"They're certainly smaller than my friend's Great Dane," she said.

On a recent crisp, clear afternoon, Kenneth's 29-inch stallion, Toyland Tiddley Winks, could have passed for a full-sized horse as he galloped, squealed and playfully kicked up his heels.

"They don't know they're miniature," said the ranch's trainer, Lloyd Reed, who has spent his career training regular-sized horses. "They still think like a big horse."

Since summer, Kenneth has traveled around the United States and as far as England to collect her 30 miniatures, which include three stallions, a few geldings and several mares.

"I'm studying genetics," she said. "It's quite complicated, really."

Kenneth's studying will pay off this spring, she hopes, when a handful of her mares give birth to foals from Toyland Tiddley Winks, whose father, Balloon's Buckeroo, sold for $100,000.

"Balloon's Buckeroo is known for producing top-quality babies," Kenneth said, "and this little guy is going to do the same thing for me."

But Kenneth didn't come to Central Oregon to raise horses. A spacious, rustic house on Winston Ranch with a picture-window view of the Three Sisters drew her to Bend two years ago from Minneapolis, where she managed apartment buildings.

"I never had anything more than a dog," she noted, but life in Bend changed all that and she raised sheep for a while.

"I went through the lambing process," she said. "I gave shots. And this is from a city girl."

However, she gave up on the sheep business and decided she would raise animals "you didn't eat."

She bought an Arabian horse, hired a trainer and learned how to ride. And then she heard about the miniatures.

Miniatures were originally raised in Europe as pets for the children of royalty, Kenneth said. Some were brought to the United States from Europe in the early 1900s and used in mines to haul coal cars.

Today, there are fewer than 15,000 in the United States, compared to 2 million to 3 million regular-sized horses in the country.

The breed appealed to her, she said, because they offer an investment incentive to the mini-rancher.

There is nothing miniature in the worth of the small horses, with the foals and horses demanding prices ranging from $1,000 to $10,000. On the average, the miniature costs more to purchase than regular-sized horses, Kenneth said.

The savings come from the upkeep of the small animals, because they don't eat much, don't take up much space and don't require shoeing.

But the breed's loving, gentle nature and overall smallness were what really appealed to Kenneth, she said, adding that the horses are perfect for her "golden years."

"They're not as hard on the body; they're rather docile," she said. "These little guys are so nice and easy to handle. You don't have to worry about being kicked or tromped on."

Her trainer agrees miniatures are loving little rascals, but said "a good kick on the kneecap" from one of the small horses can hurt. "But they won't step on your feet near as hard," Reed added.

While miniatures are too small to ride, the horses can be driven, shown at halter and can compete over jumps with the owner guiding them with a lead rope.

Besides being small—they can't be taller than 38 inches—breed standards demand that the horses possess the fine body structure of their larger counterparts.

"You see, you want them to be perfect, with a good top line, straight legs and a nice head," Kenneth said.

Her finer minis will be housed in a recently completed "mini-barn," an older barn on the property that Kenneth converted into a nine-stall show stable.

"I woke up in the middle of the night and realized I had this building," she said. "I got up, got some graph paper and laid it out. I had never seen a show barn before."

The heated building features a roped-off show ring for exhibiting the horses. The extravagant barn also includes an office, veterinary room, laundry room for the horses' blankets and a cozy viewing room overlooking the ring, complete with elegant furniture and a stereo.

Commentary

Paragraphs
1 and 2.   —The writer grabs your interest with a description of unusual animals which she purposely doesn't yet identify.

Paragraph 3.   —A direct quote further peaks your curiosity, and then the story's topic is identified. (Note: Editors generally agree that a direct quote early in the story lends to its human interest appeal or grabs the reader's attention.)

Paragraph 4.   —Kenneth's business is specified, and an important fact is revealed: how small the horses are. (Note: In many publications, journalists use the subject's last name only on second and following references. And, courtesy titles, such as "Mrs.," are often avoided. I prefer this method. However, if you're writing about two people with the same surname, you could use first names only on second and following references to prevent confusion. And, to be informal, you can also use first names only on second and following references if you're writing about a child. Also Note: Editors prefer mention of the interviewee's age.)

Paragraph 5.   —The writer clarifies how small the horses are by quoting Kenneth who makes a good comparison. (A direct quote is often set apart in a single paragraph to make it more readable to the eye.)

Paragraph 6. —The writer's good observation allows the reader to formulate a mental image.

Paragraph 7. —The writer includes an interesting quote from another key figure involved.

Paragraph 8. —More necessary specifics on the business, including the interesting fact of where the owner obtains the horses. And, as this writer does, when dealing with specific kinds of things—in this case, horses—you must offer a breakdown.

Paragraphs 9 through 11. —The writer follows with facts on the owner's goal for the business, which is an important question to ask any business owner.

Paragraphs 12 through 16. —Background information on Kenneth is woven into the story. It's best, as this writer does, to include this information in the middle of the story— right when the reader begins to wonder about it—rather than save it until the last few paragraphs. Also, as this writer inquires, it's important when interviewing people, to ask how they got started in what they do. In paragraph 14, with "And this is from a city girl," the writer misses the opportunity to follow with a comment on what tone of voice the interviewee used when making this statement. The writer could have specified that Kenneth said this "with a sense of wonder," for example.

Paragraph 17. —Background is given on the origin of miniature horses, as the reader needs to know. As the writer does, it is necessary to specifically attribute facts which aren't commonly known, to the person who says them. In this case, the writer says, "Kenneth said," so the reader is clear on where the authoritative information is from.

Paragraph 18. —Good comparison of how rare miniatures are in this country. The reader needs to know such specifics. As this writer makes clear, one must always put numbers into their proper perspective with a comparison which readers can relate to.

*Paragraphs 19
through 21.*   —As this writer does, in a feature, you must ask the interviewee why he/she is involved in a particular activity. In this case, it's partly the investment incentive. But, perhaps these paragraphs should have followed paragraph 11. Also, it's confusing why Balloon's Buckeroo sold for $100,000 when other miniatures sell for $1,000 to $10,000. Further, in paragraph 20, it could be specified how much regular-size horses cost. In paragraph 21, it also might have been interesting had the writer specified what the horses eat and how much.

*Paragraph 22
through 24.*   —These paragraphs could have followed paragraph 18, with a transition such as, "As for Kenneth's primary attraction to the breed, she found their loving, gentle nature..." (Note: In every feature about a person with an interesting job or activity, the writer should include what the person likes and dislikes about it. This writer doesn't mention the latter, though it's good to include, because no matter how much someone enjoys what they do, there are always drawbacks to it.)

Paragraphs 25
through 27.   —Perhaps the information here could have been integrated earlier in the story (i.e., from the 4th through 7th paragraphs), since the reader wonders about this information from the beginning.

Paragraphs 28
through 30.   —You finish the story perhaps wanting to know more specifics about the extravagant stable. However, the writer does well to end with this information since it is the least important in the story. As you'll learn in subsequent chapters, journalistic articles are structured to start with the important information, and work downward to the least vital.

News Story Comparison

Now that you're familiar with feature stories, let's compare them to a news story. Following are the first few paragraphs of a news story. (By the way, they are fabricated.) You will note their explicit, straightforward style—a blow-by-blow account with facts, figures, and names. These "grafs" (paragraphs) differ from the casual style of a flowing feature:

Six-foot deep floodwaters Monday destroyed about 2,500 homes in Montague, forcing about 4,000 to evacuate. The storm, which closed roads and highways, left three dead and 32 missing.

Among victims in the storm's series, which began five days ago, was a helicopter crewman killed Saturday while trying to evacuate an elderly heart attack victim.

Gov. Bud Kupp, who has declared a state of emergency, flew over the town Monday to survey flooding and said the destruction was "the worst I've seen in this state in 23 years."

The cost of damage to roads and highways alone is estimated at $8 million, according to Duff County Emergency Services Director David Mills.

An Incentive

Don't you think writing features would be much more fun than writing news stories? Feature writing isn't tedious, because the fact gathering doesn't get complicated and overwhelm you, as news stories sometimes do.

So, keep reading and master this simple craft.

III

Locating Article Ideas

You should know the practical ways which busy staff journalists use to locate story ideas on a daily basis.

The most common way is to read area newspapers and magazines for press releases. These are announcements, a few paragraphs long, about events and people connected with them. Besides finding press releases in community and metropolitan newspapers and magazines, check local tabloids (half-size papers), neighborhood papers, or special interest ones like those for senior citizens.

For example, if there is a press release about an upcoming festival which says that among performers will be John Lowe, a local magician, that might be a story idea for you. You could interview Lowe before the festival and mention in your story when he'll be performing. Or, you could keep his name on file for a future interview.

Another way of orienting yourself to what's happening in your area is to read meeting notice or social club column listings in local publications. Here, you'll discover many new special interest groups. For example, I once read a meeting notice about a support group for divorced parents who didn't have custody of their children. The note included the name of a contact person and his phone number. I contacted him and mentioned my possible interest in writing a story about his group. I attended a meeting, got quotes from a few members, and wrote about the group's purpose and goals, along with including facts and opinions on the problems which non-custodial parents face.

Following are other ways to locate story ideas:

• *Read Local Columnists*

They offer tidbits on upcoming events or interesting people.

• *Read Newspaper Ads*

For example, you can find ads about interesting businesses. I once read an ad about a person who wanted to purchase memorabilia from World War I. I contacted him for an interview and wrote an interesting feature about his interest in collecting helmets and guns. (If someone doesn't have a business address, but is home-based, you should take a friend along to check out the business, rather than visit a stranger's house. And, before you see what he has to offer, it's wise not to mention your interest in writing an article—just pose as a prospective buyer. After you've determined it's worth a story, announce your intentions.)

- *Read the Phone Book's Yellow Pages*

First, consider your interests and think of what you might like to learn about. Are you interested in learning about social service organizations, for example? Scan the phone book, and you'll discover things you never knew existed. If you find an organization which sounds interesting or unusual, ask to be sent information about its purpose and function, and then decide if there's a story in it.

- *Read Newsletters/Brochures*

If you receive newsletters from local organizations such as the art museum, or see brochures about organizations at the library, keep your eyes open for notices about interesting classes, exhibits, or events connected with them which you could write about.

Some public libraries print a pamphlet which lists local resource groups and organizations with names of contact people. Visit the Information or Adult Services Department of your public library.

- *Places You Often Visit*

If you go to a fair, for example, and see exhibits you like, get the names of local craftspeople for future reference. Also, if you're shopping and see items which are locally handmade, ask for the name of the craftsperson and how to contact him. If he's not listed in the phone book and the proprietors won't reveal his number, then leave your name with them and have them contact the craftsperson for you.

- *Read Alumni Magazines*

I've discovered many feature ideas about local people from reading notes and stories about them in alumni magazines. After interviewing them, I've crafted my own stories for local general interest publications.

- *Consider all Your Contacts*

Who do you know who is interesting? A neighbor? Who do your friends know who is interesting? Who do your relatives know? Get story ideas from other people, particularly those who are actively involved in the community and who know a lot of people.

Whether you remember it or not, recently, you've probably been told about someone who would make a good story. From now on, pay attention when people mention others. If you hear of someone who might be a possibility, maybe you could be introduced to him, if you are shy about calling cold. If not, call and introduce yourself as a freelance writer.

Embarrassed about going out on your first interview? Try something simple like writing about a club or group you're connected with. However, don't make it a first person story. Leave yourself out of it by quoting other group members.

And, what if you've just moved to a new region and don't have many contacts? Do you have children in the local schools? If so, are they doing any interesting projects? For example, is their class raising money for needy people? If it is, interview the teacher and the kids about the project. Find out why they are involved and what their goal is.

* *Read Many Publications for Ideas*

If you read an article in the local paper and think you could do a better job with it, do the interview, write the story, and sell it to a regionally or nationally-circulated publication, if applicable. For example, I had a student who read in the local paper about a dog who did unusual tricks at a flea market each week. My student, being a dog lover, often read *Dog Fancy,* a nationally-circulated magazine. She crafted a good story about the dog for the magazine and got it published.

The story included quotes from the dog's owner and information about how he trained it.

When I read publications in other areas, I often obtain ideas which I can apply to my area. For example, if I read a newspaper in a different region and see a feature about someone there who builds canoes, I may try to locate someone nearby who does it. Be curious and keep informing yourself of what's happening elsewhere.

• *Running into Ideas by Accident*

You run into ideas all the time, even if you stay at home. I had a 200-foot poplar tree chopped down in my backyard. After observing the logger, I struck up a conversation with him because he and his strenuous job intrigued me— working at dizzying heights with a heavy saw and lowering enormous logs with ropes to the ground. I ended up writing a feature about this unique man who, I found, had broken his back in an airplane crash a few years before, and who was told he would never even walk again. So, the moral is, always be talking to people!

Another personal example of running into ideas by accident, is when I was once looking through a national directory of artists to find the address of a long-lost friend in Missouri. Out of curiosity, I became sidetracked and looked under the directory's section with the names and descriptions of artists in my state. I read about an

interesting watercolor painter whom I contacted
and ended up writing a feature about.

Concluding Tidbits

Now, I've given some suggestions to get you
started in obtaining ideas. Always keep a file or clip
possible ideas from publications, even if they may
seem to be remote possibilities. You may not be
interested in using them now, but maybe they'll look
more appealing in a few months. Also, spend a few
minutes sometime and brainstorm. How about the
topic of Flamenco dancing? Look through the
Yellow Pages of the phone book and maybe you'll
find a Flamenco teacher to interview, and you could
also observe her class in action to formulate a good
story.

What about a seasonal story? Consider this as an
idea for a feature which could run in a publication
for April Fool's Day: "Office Gags." You could
interview people who've executed fun or unusual
jokes on others at their workplace.

You should open yourself to the possibility that
there's a feature idea in almost anything. Once you
have an idea, ask yourself: Would this be interesting
to write about and why?

You could even be like Charles Kuralt, network
television newsman and author, who travels the
backroads of America and runs into interesting
people (auctioneer, singing mailman, etc.) and towns

to report on. (See the appendix for one of his books.)

Whatever you choose to write about, keep your story ideas simple. With a freelancer, editors feel they have no control over fact gathering since they can't monitor you as they would a staff writer. They tend to trash freelance stories of a controversial nature or those which require a lot of complicated fact gathering which they can't take time to verify. So, especially in the beginning, select ideas which make light reading, such as people stories.

IV

Interviewing Techniques

You've got a story idea. How do you handle the interview? Can you do it by telephone?

Never! It's important with a feature story that you meet the interviewee and observe him in his environment. Was he smoking a pipe during the interview? Were the office walls cluttered with funny posters? If these points are significant, you'll include them in your story.

I once interviewed a publisher of Christian books who operated from his basement with a printing press and a few sticks of old furniture. I wrote these facts in my story.

Before the interview, when you phone to arrange for it, you should tell the interviewee which publication you plan on submitting the story to. You want to determine if he has already appeared in that publication, regarding the area of his life you are interested in writing about. Say, for example, you are interested in writing about him and his business.

If someone already wrote a story about his business for that publication a few years ago, then it's fine to proceed with setting up an interview, if he says major developments have occurred in his business since then. If, however, a story appeared about his business in that publication only a few months ago, you should either interview him for another publication or forget doing the interview.

You must prepare for the interview by devising a list of at least 20 questions. Go to the interview with those questions. If you don't, regardless of how great your memory is, you're sure to forget to ask some important questions. I usually ask about 35 to 40 questions and spend 1½ to 2 hours at the interview. I avoid imposing on the interviewee, however, by mentioning when I phone him about how long the interview will last.

Besides the questions, be prepared by dressing well. The interviewee is anxious to meet you because he doesn't know who you are. You must look somewhat professional, because you don't want to appear as a starving writer.

"What if I'm going to be doing an interview on a farm?" you ask. "Wouldn't good clothes be inappropriate?"

No one says you need to walk through a cow pasture in a three-piece suit. But, on the other hand, you're not a farmer, so you wouldn't show up in bib overalls. In this case, use your common sense and try corduroy slacks, for example. (However, if you were participating in the action and writing a first person experience story, you could, of course, show up in denims.)

Interviews can be disappointing, but there are ways to prevent this. If you are interviewing someone with an interesting job or hobby, for example, he may not know how to communicate what he does. Or, to him, it's become routine and he's lost sight of how it might interest others. Or, maybe the interviewee is shy or nervous. So, from the minute you walk in the door, put him at ease. Tell him, for example, that he has a nice house or office. Talk about something off the subject. For example, if you see a picture of his children, ask where they attend school, and comment on yours.

After small talk, begin with simple questions, those which don't call for much reflection, to break the ice. Sometimes background questions will do it. For example, ask when and how he got started doing what he does, or if anyone in his family does it, too. I once interviewed an airline pilot. He said that no one in his family flew airplanes, but that since childhood he'd always been fascinated with them and he built model ones. Later, as a young man in the Air Force, he decided his future career would be as a commercial pilot.

With a lengthy interview, you give the interviewee much time to think of thoughtful answers. Don't, however, let the interviewee digress and turn it into a five-hour interview. If he starts to digress, put him on track by saying you're interested in further pursuing a certain area.

Treat that person with respect, because you've selected him as an interviewee. Be patient, even if he's a poor communicator, and ask him to be specific. Don't settle for vague or ambiguous statements. If you're not sure you understand something, stop, and ask for clarification or for an example. And don't settle for plain "yes" or "no" answers. Two good words to follow up with are "why" or "how."

If you are interviewing someone with an interesting hobby, for example, besides background questions, include ones like:

• Why do you do it? Why do you enjoy it?

• How much of your time does the hobby require?

• When do you find time for it? Do you sneak out during the night and go into your workshop while the family is asleep? (In your story, state what part of town the home/workshop is located in—specific address is not necessary, if interviewee's privacy is a concern.)

• Is it an expensive hobby?

• What skills are needed to do it? Can anyone do it?

- Explain the step-by-step process of how the hobby is done. (If an item is created, describe what tools or machinery are used to create it.)

- If the person produces an item for sale, what is its price? And, how is the item marketed?

- Ask: What do your friends or family think of your hobby? (A direct quote from this other party would even be appropriate.)

- Ask: What is your age? (Generally, editors want you to include someone's age. The exception is if you are interviewing movie stars, since they tend to lie about it. When you ask for someone's age, if you think he's untruthful, don't include it in your story.)

- Ask: What is your occupation?

As for other queries, ask yourself: What do I want to know about this person? That's what your reader probably wants to know.

Unless you're writing about a famous person, you usually don't need to do any advance research. If the person is famous, go to the library and use the index of major magazines and newspapers to find the articles which have been written about him. A famous person, of course, would be insulted if you didn't already know something about him. With a famous person, ask personal facts about him: where he grew up, where he went to school, what his parents did for a living, if he has children, etc.

If you plan on writing about a topic that's unfamiliar to you like blacksmithing, there's no need to research the topic before interviewing a blacksmith. Just ask the blacksmith basic questions on your mind which any layperson would ask, including how he does the work and specifically what methods and tools are used.

During the interview, write down all answers to questions which your interviewee gives. Don't rely on your memory, because you can't even afford to slip up on one fact. Devise your own shorthand of abbreviations. If the interviewee talks too fast, ask him to slow down or repeat something.

Beginning writers always wonder if they should tape interviews. I discourage this for a few basic reasons. First, in feature stories, you want to give interviewees every opportunity to reflect and give good, coherent answers. Taping, however, tends to make interviewees feel pressured to respond quickly. There's also the subsequent problem of having to tediously transcribe a long tape. Finally, there's the possibility of a tape malfunction, and if this happened, you couldn't very well impose on the interviewee by asking for another lengthy interview.

Note-taking, therefore, is best. Always bring an extra pencil in case one quits. It's disruptive and unprofessional to ask the interviewee for one.

As for ethics, if an interviewee asks you not to print a fact, follow his wishes. Strangely enough, I've found that interviewees usually ask you not to include some trivial fact, which if printed, would not be embarrassing in the least. If this is the case, I ask the interviewee why he doesn't want it printed. If I don't see a problem with it, and the fact is relevant, I try to persuade him to let me print it.

(Another ethics point, is that you should never exploit interviewees. For example, sometimes features are written about social problems, such as wife-battering, etc. I don't interview people immediately after they've experienced a trauma, when they are in a terrible emotional state. Afterwards, they regret they publicized their case. Put yourself in the interviewees' shoes, and wait until the dust has settled. Be a sensitive interviewer!)

At the end of the interview, ask the interviewee if he wants to add anything. Also, briefly glance through your notes to see if any facts are vague or quotes are unclear. At this time, get them clarified. It's also a good idea to tell the interviewee that you may be calling to clarify any points while you're writing the story.

Sometimes, interviewees ask if they can read the story before you submit it. This is not a good idea, because as a writer, you shouldn't be seeking their approval for your writing style and judgment. When the airline pilot I interviewed asked if he could read my story before it was published, I jokingly replied, "Can I fly your airplane?" The point is, it's your job to be a good writer. However, reassure the interviewee that you'll certainly be accurate with your facts.

Immediately after getting home from the interview, review your notes in detail while what the interviewee said is still fresh in your mind. Fill in little notations to clarify some of the scribblings you made.

A Hypothetical Interview

Now that you know some basics, try a hypothetical interview. Pretend that tomorrow you'll interview an interstate trucker who hauls cars cross-country. Think of at least 20 questions, in any order, that you'd like to ask. Then, compare your list with mine.

Interview

1) Observe the trucker. Is he a big man? Ask how tall he is and how much he weighs.

2) What does he talk like?

3) Observe his truck. (I hope when you "scheduled" the interview, you said you wanted to see his truck, too.) What color is it? Does he have a name for it? What's the inside like? The sleeping area? Does it have a refrigerator? Does it look like a motel on wheels? Ask how many tons it weighs.

4) How old is the trucker? Married? Kids?

5) How long has he been trucking?

6) When did he first drive a truck? (Did he drive a pick-up as a kid on his grandfather's farm?)

7) How much time does he spend away from home in a given month?

8) Is it stressful work? What are the pressures? Is it competitive? How? Is he on a tight schedule? Ask for an example.

9) How many hours at a time does he spend behind the wheel without rest?

10) What does he like about his job?

11) What does he dislike about it? Does he hate loading and unloading cars?

12) How many tons does the freight usually weigh?

13) Is it lonely driving? If so, how does he combat loneliness? Does he sing to himself? What songs?

14) How does he dress when he's on the road?

15) How long does he usually sleep each night when he's on the road?

16) What qualifications does a trucker need? Ask about government licensing and course of instruction.

17) What did he do before he became a trucker?

18) How much does he earn? (If he doesn't want to answer this, ask about pay range for truckers.)

19) Has he ever had a close call? If so, ask for a description. (This might make a good direct quote.)

20) How long does he expect to continue trucking?

A Success Story

One of my students decided to follow through with the previous exercise and interview a trucker. Being brave on her first interview, she went to a truck stop and asked the diner's waitress to introduce her to a regular trucker-patron.

The trucker was flattered that he would be interviewed, as most interviewees are. During the interview, he took her through a tour of his "Blue

Lady." The interview lasted four hours (quite long), but both were engrossed in the topic.

It was worth the time, since the story was published in a local newspaper.

V

Writing the Feature

Before we get into the structure of the feature story and how to organize it, let's begin with the lighter details of working with sentences.

Part 1) Language

Lead Sentences/Paragraphs

Journalists, whether news or feature writers, begin a story with a snappy lead sentence. This is achieved, for example, through a pun or other device to grab the readers' attention and to encourage them to continue. As for a pun, if you wanted to write a feature about someone who collects matchbook covers, for example, you might begin with: *Lisa Elmer's hobby is matchless.*

Besides puns, let's look at lead sentences which indirectly describe people in their environments, and hint at the story's topic. A story about a nature lover could begin with: *He lived in a rickety shack with creaking gaps between the floorboards, some sealed with acorns for two squirrels which often scurried through the front door.*

Let's consider this lead to a hypothetical feature about corporate board members: *Oblivious to surrounding skyscrapers, they sat upright in semi-padded oak chairs in a plushly-carpeted, soft gray suite.*

Besides lead sentences, let's consider a hypothetical lead paragraph, one which hints at the feature's topic and prods the reader on:

Lonna's pregnancy test was positive. Sue and Billy Joe got lovey-dovey. And Tim told Mary Lou their romance is over.

Did you guess that the above lead paragraph could introduce a soap opera story?

Here's another lead paragraph which grabs you:

It's 5 p.m. and humid, and Sumner Heights is alive. Along Fuller Avenue, near the elevated train tracks, the end of another long week in Green Island is celebrated with Latin flare. Salsa music flows from cafes and storefronts, and seven teenagers, spiked by the beat as they pass by, pulsate into loose-limbed dancing. Seconds later, they soulfully strut toward the next sidewalk-fest.

The above lead paragraph, which is fabricated, describes a Latin neighborhood and could be used to introduce a story about Latin restaurants and other food outlets. For a story of this kind, this lead would probably be more effective than using one which starts right in discussing food, because it teases you to read on and discover the story's topic. Personally, I favor these lead paragraphs which create a mood or describe an environment in which a story takes place.

Parts of Speech/Comparisons

To liven up your writing, use verbs, adjectives, similes, and metaphors which create powerful images. You don't, however, have to be a poet or creative person to write features. Most journalists aren't creative people per se, but technicians who gather and arrange facts in a colorful way. If they were really creative, chances are, they'd be writing poetry or novels. There are exceptions, of course. George Orwell, the novelist who wrote *1984*, was also a journalist.

You can easily select verbs which contribute to the description you're trying to convey. When you write, you may naturally tend to first think of a general verb. The next step, however, is to become more specific with a descriptive verb which demonstrates your good observation skills. Think of how someone is doing something. For example, if you're writing about Mary Jones who models clothes, don't say, "She walked across the stage." Ask yourself how she walked. Did she glide, for example?

Let's take another example. You could write, "The concert-goers reached the auditorium." But, this is better: *The concert-goers scrambled to the auditorium.*

Other examples:

You first think of the sentence, "He chewed his food." Then, you should ask yourself how he chewed his food. This leads you to specific verbs such as *nibble, devour,* or *savor.*

Take another sentence: "He moved through the woods." How did he move? Did he *dash, skip, trudge, stroll, ramble, tramp,* or *amble?*

Let's do the same with adjectives. Take a general adjective such as "bad," as in the sentence, "The movie was bad." Then, ask yourself: How was it bad? Was it *boring, foolish, ridiculous,* or *unpleasant?*

Adjectives allow your story's tone to be subjective with your perspectives. For example, if you think the interviewee is vivacious, describe him as such.

With adjectives, strive to appeal to the reader through his senses. Describing the person's physical features is often relevant. If you're writing about a jockey, the story would lack information if you didn't describe his body's build, because there are regulations governing his height and weight. If you're writing about a model, is she blonde? Blue-eyed? Of course, include her height and weight.

Describe how the person is dressed, if relevant. For example, if you're writing about someone who fights forest fires, what kind of clothes does he/she wear on the job? Are they drab-looking?

As for similes and metaphors, let's start with the former first, since they are often easier to create. A simile is a comparison of two things made by using the words "like" or "as."

If, for example, you're describing baseball fans exiting the stadium, you should ask yourself: The baseball fans are exiting like what? Are they like a herd of cattle exiting a fence? If so, your simile would include that comparison preceded by a specific verb: *The baseball fans stampeded from the stadium like a herd of cattle.*

A metaphor identifies two different objects or ideas based on some aspect of likeness which both possess. Unlike a simile, there is no use of "like" or "as," so apparently the comparison is a literally impossible claim. For example, if the rock fans are wild, your metaphor could be: *The rock fans are wild horses.*

As a writer, choose whether you are more comfortable using similes or metaphors. If you're familiar with Erma Bombeck, syndicated columnist, one reason you probably enjoy her writing is because she uses comparisons which you can relate to.

Perhaps it's a good idea to keep lists of similes and metaphors as they come to you, as seasoned writers often do.

Let's look at some similes and metaphors which I've created:

- *The bald man's scalp beamed like a semi-licked lollipop. (simile)*

- *The mud stuck to the hill like caramel to an apple. (simile)*

- *As she stirred, the cold drink was a rippling emerald sea. (metaphor)*

- *The little girl is a twinkling star. (metaphor)*

General Description

To brighten your description, sharpen your observation skills to the point of concentrating on each detail of action.

Consider these examples where concentration is clearly at work:

- The employee slammed the manager's office door with her head high, and one clenched fist suggested indignation.

- The elderly invalid scanned the room with disdain, squinting through her monocle.-

- The toddler's eyes rose to Big Red, the velour devil, on the top toy shelf. There were papier-mâché angels, on either side of it, hanging by thread from the ceiling. (Note: Journalists often put proper names before the description of who or what it is. Therefore, Big Red, precedes the velour devil. Also, journalists usually avoid putting quotation marks around names such as Big Red, even though they are not typical proper names.)

Part 2) Content

Reporting Facts

In reporting facts, be thorough. Journalistic writing is complete and explicit. After you've written a story, there shouldn't be questions in readers' minds about the topic. So, never assume your readers know the answer to something.

Identify the basic "who, what, when, wheres." If you're writing about a person, what town does the person live in? If you're writing about a local organization, what street is it located on? Include the street number, too.

Spell out all facts to possible questions. For example, if you're writing a story about someone who lives in a houseboat, don't make a statement like "Living in a houseboat is expensive," unless you specify what the costs are in relation to house living. Also, you should realize that what is expensive to one person, isn't always expensive to another. So, avoid vague statements.

If, for example, you write about Mary McHugh who volunteers at many organizations including the local Red Cross, what specific tasks does she do?

As another example, if you're writing about a handicapped person, and you mention that he has faced and overcome many challenges in living alone and caring for himself, specify what those living skill challenges are and how he copes.

Never write in generalities. Bring the story to life with specific examples and interesting tidbits.

One of my students wrote a feature about a popular knitting teacher in town. During the interview, the knitting teacher had mentioned that she had 250 sweaters in her wardrobe that she'd knitted, so my student included this fact in the story. The questions that came to my mind, which the student didn't include the answers to in her story, were: Where did the teacher find the space in her home to store all those sweaters? How much drawer space did she have?

My point is, always be thinking, always be questioning. And, never overlook interesting, curious tidbits in the content.

I read a story in a newspaper, which was a naturally good, lively idea, but which turned out to be a disappointment because the content was lacking. The story was about high school students and the interior decorating of their school lockers. The writer missed his chance to make the story interesting by not only failing to specifically describe the locker decor, but also by not describing the personalities and their reasoning behind the decor.

For example, one student displayed a spoon collection in his locker. But, the writer didn't specify what kind it was, and where the student collected the spoons from. About another student's locker, the writer merely said there was Elvis Presley memorabilia. Of course, anyone would be curious to find out what kind it was. I also wondered about the students behind the decor. The writer mentioned that a high school senior had a politically-oriented locker decor with photos of democratic politicians such as the late John F. Kennedy. I wondered about how this student became interested in Kennedy, who was in office before the student was born. Did he get interested in Kennedy from studying about him in school, or were his parents Kennedy followers? And, did the student plan to study political science in college? Basically, I found that human interest elements were lacking in the story.

I also read a simple, informational feature in a metropolitan paper which lacked reporting of basic facts. The feature was about a youth Explorer program where participants worked with the local police force, patrolling with officers in order to get a taste of a police career. In it, the writer answered these basic questions about the program: when it was founded, who was eligible to join, how many kids participated, what tasks they did while on the job, and the program's objectives. It also included direct quotes from the police officer who oversaw the program and from a few of the kids participating about their image of police officers as helpers in the community. It even included, as any good story should, both sides of the issue—in this case, that not everyone who participated ended up deciding that a career in police work was for them.

However, the story did lack information about the specific training the teen-agers received from the police. I wondered, for example, if they received classroom training before being able to go out on patrol with the police. And, the story did not answer the facts about how much time each week or month participants were expected to devote to the program, nor if they were evaluated by the police for their work. Further, the story lacked good direct quotes from the kids concerning any interesting experiences they'd had while patrolling with the police. This story not only lacked basic information, but without interesting quotes from the kids, it also lacked color!

If you leave facts to the readers' imaginations, you're not writing journalistically.

Say, for example, you're writing about a friend who is a hang glider and you already know something about how he does it. Don't forget to include basic facts your readers might ask. As a beginner, there are often problems in writing about topics you know something about, because you overlook reporting facts that are obvious to you, but not to the average reader.

When you write for a mass publication like your local newspaper or a general interest magazine, assume your reader is totally ignorant of the subject. However, in writing for trade publications for peers in a particular field, you obviously would assume they had basic knowledge of the subject.

Although I've hammered away at being specific and explaining facts thoroughly, be sure not to repeat facts. It's often common for beginning writers to basically state the same fact using different words.

Another mistake that beginners make is to forget to define terms. If, for example, you are covering Down's Syndrome, then a non-clinical definition and description of the syndrome are needed early in the story. Not everyone is clear on what this syndrome and its characteristics are, so describe it in terms laypeople can comprehend.

Use common sense. Define a term, if there's any doubt in your mind that readers don't know its meaning. And, be sure to use terms and words correctly. Be careful not to mislabel people or things. When I was in the editor's seat at a magazine, a freelancer submitted an article which made reference to a 27-year-old "girl." For an adult female, the term is "woman."

Still another mistake that beginning feature writers often make, is that they are so enthusiastic about the people or organizations they're writing about, that the feature story sounds more like an advertisement or promotional piece. Try to avoid this if you are writing for general interest publications, rather than public relations house organs.

Reporting Direct Quotes

As we've seen, writing in a clear, colorful way is important.

Now, let's carry this further with the use of direct quotes. Generally, editors agree that a direct quote, used early in the story, helps to grab the reader's attention. The first direct quote could be used as high as the second or third paragraph. However, editors generally feel that a direct quote in the first paragraph, especially if it's a long one, may confuse the reader.

Direct quotes should be used in primarily three situations:

1) If someone says something in an interesting or colorful way which reveals a facet of their personality.

2) If one gives an opinion which would lose something if you put it in your own words.

3) If one says something very important which you wanted your reader to pay particular attention to.

Never quote someone on a fact which you could easily put into your own words. For example, if Jack Dunn is 44 years old and single, don't quote him as saying, "I'm 44 years old and single."

If, however, Dunn said, "I'm 44 years old, single and proud of it," that merits a direct quote because it reveals something about his personality.

If a person uses comprehensible slang, don't clean up the quote. Use it, unless you feel that he didn't mean to, and that he slipped up with poor grammar.

For example, if someone speaks in a colorful rural dialect, quote him in his style.

Generally, don't fill in words when you're quoting someone. If the interviewee said, "Been a cowboy now, going on ten years," you wouldn't insert the beginning word "I've."

However, if the quote's meaning isn't completely clear unless missing words are supplied, you could put them in parentheses. For example, if you asked George Trent to comment on a family business which his wife and mother run, and he said, "She's a creative woman with much potential," this would be confusing. Is he talking about his wife or mother? For clarity, you could insert, "She (my wife) is a creative..."

It's best not to have your story overflow with direct quotes. They should be sprinkled like salt, otherwise you lose control of your story and it becomes a record of quotes.

Also, remember to avoid using direct quotes when the interviewee is obviously boasting about himself or his organization. Perhaps in this case, you could instead use a direct quote from an objective person such as a client.

Part 3) Story Analysis

Read the following story about autism which has major problems with content and style. The story is fabricated and contains fictitious names and places. Parts of it were drawn from various students' papers. Take notes as you read and mark flaws. Decide what more could have been included had the story been well-developed. Had you done this interview, what would you have been interested in finding out? Also, number the 21 paragraphs to facilitate reading the commentary which follows.

Beware: You should never fabricate a feature story. I have done so only to elaborate on a variety of errors, as a teaching tool.

This is the story:

Joan Katzen mops the kitchen floor while seven children sit in the dining room and finish eating their snacks.

When snack time is through, Katzen emerges and tells Martin DeFrancisco to eat his untouched dried apricots.

"I really detest dried fruit," the boy says. "I despise it." He throws the bag of apricots across the room, hitting the wall.

Katzen retrieves the bag and throws it back.

"Martin, either eat your apricots or march right up to your room," she says.

The boy first examines the bag and then eats the apricots.

The youngster, 10, has autism, a neurological disorder which leaves victims unaware of their surroundings, unable to do some basic daily living skills, and impaired in speech, according to professionals.

Katzen, 27, is a "houseparent" whose duties —besides caring for the autistic children, ages

8 to 13—include housekeeping, laundry, cooking, and buying groceries. Together, they live in this group home, a single-family residence on Meadowbrook Drive in Fulton.

The home, which opened June 3, is owned by Helping Hand People, Inc., a private non-profit group supported by state funds and private contributions, projected at $920,000 this year.

Katzen is among 16 staff members who work shifts and teach the children skills from brushing their teeth and combing their hair, to dusting furniture. On weekends, the staff takes the youngsters to shopping centers, fairs, zoos, and beaches. During weekdays, for a few hours, the children receive varied instruction at Helping Hand School in Lansfield.

The learning of basic skills is gradual, says Todd Dodsen, the home's executive director. He says only a few of these afflicted children will eventually lead normal lives. For the majority of residents, the staff's objective is to socialize them, so they can go home to live with their parents. Dodsen says, on the average, the children will stay at the group home for 21 months.

"We feel it's really important for the youngsters to have daily chores," Dodsen says. "Martin wipes the kitchen counter every day after meals. It's become a routine, and routine is essential for these kids. Martin could have done this chore when he was living with his mom and dad, but he simply refused to do it. Instead, he would punch, bite, and scream at them. We prodded Martin for two months before he would clean the counter without resistance."

Melissa DeFrancisco, the boy's mother, is especially appreciative of the group home because of her son's progress.

"Before Martin came to Helping Hand, whenever Jack, my husband, and I would tell him to do anything, even just a minor thing, he would fight until our fingers would bleed and our arms and legs had bruises," DeFrancisco says. "It was hard for us to deal with this behavior."

Before the home opened, the mother had little time or energy for other duties, such as running her household, doing errands, and raising her younger child, Billy, age 4.

"When Martin lived with us, and I would take him somewhere, he would seem nervous in all public places," the young woman explains. "When we went to the department store, for instance, Martin would always act up: he'd roam around touching all the items on the shelf, plop himself on the floor, or stand with his back against a bare wall. It was strange."

As his mother watches, the boy has now finished eating. He begins singing with words which can hardly be heard or comprehended. After a few minutes, he runs out of the dining room.

"Did you ask permission to leave this room?" Katzen shouts.

He stops, turns, and replies, "May I go to the bathroom?"

Katzen nods. As he scoots, he yells, "Thank you very much." Katzen smiles.

The group home, the only one of its kind in the state, may be shut down if a lawsuit filed by its neighbors is won. The neighbors claim that the home was improperly granted a permit to operate.

Commentary

It appears that with this story, "the writer" didn't do a good job. First, the topic of autism is much too complicated to be dealt with in such short form. This story should take up the space of a long magazine-type of feature, such as one appearing in a newspaper's Sunday magazine supplement, or it should be as long as a feature series (divided into a few stories) in a daily newspaper. (Each story could focus on different aspects: the various cases of autism, the program which includes the school, and interviews with the people involved such as the families.) Secondly, the information presented is vague and flawed.

Apparently, the writer limited his interview time to a rather short period, this is, snack time. The writer should have spent a day observing at the home to thoroughly report on what the children do and learn there. His description is very sketchy. Also, if he'd spent the day, he could have developed the story by observing more than just one child and describing the other children's actions, too. With a day's observation, he could have had enough material for a magazine story which can be longer than a newspaper story, and therefore, can cover more complex topics than the latter. By observing for a day, he could have written the story chronologically, and taken the reader through breakfast, activity time, lunch, etc. He could have structured the story with paragraphs stating, for example, "It's 8 a.m....It's 9 a.m.," etc.

As for content, in the seventh paragraph, for example, the writer attempts to define what autism is, and yet, his definition is so vague that it could also fit other disorders. We never learn anything about the disorder, not even statistics on how many people it affects in the United States.

As for specific feature qualities, the observation, description, and direct quotes are very uninteresting and don't illustrate what autism is.

After readers finish this story, they have a blah feeling. The writer didn't appeal to their emotions, when the topic itself is an emotionally-charged one.

Let's look at some specifics.

The writer begins by describing Martin, the autistic child, who won't eat his apricots. Martin, responding to the houseparent's statement to eat them, says, "I really detest dried fruit." Later, we find in the writer's definition of autism that autistic children are impaired in speech, and yet, from Martin's above response, it seems his speech is even sophisticated for a 10-year-old. And Martin's defiant exchange with the houseparent, when he throws the apricots, does not necessarily illustrate the behavior of an autistic child, but could apply to any child. Now, and again later in the story, when Martin asks permission to go to the bathroom, he seems aware of his surroundings. Therefore, he isn't an example of the writer's definition of autism. (Incidentally, in the eighth paragraph, the word "houseparent" shouldn't be in quotes since it isn't an unusual word or slang.)

In the ninth paragraph, the writer weaves in important facts which we wonder about: who the home belongs to and how the program supports itself.

In the tenth and twelfth paragraphs, the writer only vaguely explains what the children are taught, and the quote from the executive director is also incomplete. First, we do not find out what the children learn in school. Secondly, the director explains that Martin was trained to wipe the counter, but the reader can't assess what the child's problems are from his example. From his description, we feel that maybe the child is just an emotionally-disturbed one.

In the fourteenth and sixteenth paragraphs, when the child's mother is quoted, we still don't have an accurate picture of what autism is. In the former paragraph, she speaks of a behavior which could be that of any emotionally-disturbed child. Further, she doesn't express her frustration, as we would expect her to. And, her quote about the child touching items on the shelf and laying down on the store floor, isn't necessarily an illustration of autistic behavior, but could merely be one of a "normal" child clowning around. The writer could have questioned the mother for a more detailed description of Martin's behavior. For example, when he was on the floor, did he look unconscious? Did he eventually get up from the floor on his own? When the mother said the behavior was strange, the writer should have questioned her for an explanation on just how this behavior was strange. (If this parent wasn't a good communicator, the writer could have gotten quotes from other parents about their children.)

In the seventeenth paragraph, when the writer describes Martin "singing with words which can hardly be heard or comprehended," we want to know more. Are they words or just sounds? Does he seem to be aware of anything happening around him as he sings? Then, after this incident, he sounds "normal" and aware when he thanks the houseparent for giving him permission to leave to go to the bathroom. Is this behavior switch typical of an autistic child?

In the story's last paragraph, the writer abruptly introduces a new subject, a lawsuit, which is another story in itself. And, he just leaves us hanging after mentioning this important subject, without statements of reaction to the suit by the staff of the home and the families it serves.

After we've finished reading, we look at where the story has taken us and are even more confused than we were at the beginning.

If it had been a good story, it would have included captivating quotes from all parties concerned: parents, houseparents, executive director (and children, if possible). If the adults had been prodded for comments, they may have opened up and illustrated their emotional involvement with the situation. The adults involved seemed detached because of the writer's apparent lack of interest in the topic. To the reader, the quotes are no more personal than the objective background facts about the home. The story also lacks smooth transitions between paragraphs, as any good article needs.

As for the story as a whole...well, reader, you can certainly do better than this. Give it a try!

(Note: If you write feature stories of this kind, obtain written permission from the families to use their real names, since the topic is of a personal nature to them. Any publication which was considering your feature for publication would

want a copy of this permission. Without written permission, you and the publication could be sued for breaching confidentiality. This also applies to topics such as drug and alcohol abuse and other interviews with people when social stigma may be involved.)

Part 4) Paragraph Structure/Organization

Have you ever noticed when reading a newspaper or magazine, that the paragraphs are generally short, much shorter than those you would write in a letter, for example?

Journalists write short paragraphs because readers are usually in a hurry and don't have time to sift through long paragraphs.

Generally, in newspapers, you see two or three-sentence paragraphs. And, it's not uncommon to see a one-sentence paragraph, if it's important information that should stand out, or if it's a direct quote.

You'll find exceptions to this. If you read *The New York Times, The Wall Street Journal* and the *Los Angeles Times,* for example, you'll notice longer, magazine-style paragraphs with four or five sentences.

Whether you write for a magazine or a newspaper, don't cram too much information into a paragraph. It becomes unreadable to the eye, especially if a reader needs to scan the article again, searching for a particular fact. And, keep the most important or interesting paragraphs early in the story. You want to grab the reader's attention soon, so if you start with less interesting facts, he might not be motivated to continue.

When writing for newspapers, remember that if editors run out of space, they often cut from the story's bottom. Toward the end, taper your story with the least interesting facts, and don't count on editors running your concluding paragraph.

When writing for magazines, however, don't be as concerned with editors cutting from the bottom. They generally tend to run a story in full, if it doesn't include extraneous information, because they aren't as pressed for space as newspaper editors are. So, when writing a magazine article, conclude with a final paragraph which ties together the story.

As for paragraph organization and sequence, it's easier than you think. Freelancers often wonder if writing an outline is needed before one begins to write the story. Don't bother. Staff journalists never have time for it. Although you may have time because you're not under deadline pressure, remember that you're not writing an English composition. So, forget the outline method you learned in junior high school.

Of course, after an interview, you'll probably be overwhelmed by all the facts you've collected. Where do you begin to organize?...Simple. Basically, organize by beginning with the most interesting information which sticks out in your mind. For example, remember the trucker interview in Chapter Four? If the trucker told you about a close call he'd once had, that may strike you when you start organizing your story, and you could begin with this dramatic element.

Try this as your lead:

Joe Jackson remembers driving along the interstate at 55 miles per hour, when a Ford van crammed with drug-crazed college kids pulled out in front of him. He slammed the brakes...

In writing a feature story, the writer decides on the best pattern of organizing, starting with those facts which he feels are most important, and then working downward to less interesting information. The writer weaves in background facts throughout the story, such as in the case of the trucker story, how long the trucker has been at his job and how he became involved in this line of work.

Organization, therefore, is subjective. I might interview the same person as you did, but I may be struck in a different way by certain information, and give it a slightly different priority than you did in your story. But, in any case, important facts should not be left until the end of the story.

As for paragraph sequence, it must be clear and logical with smooth transitions. That is, create transitions between the last sentence of one paragraph and the first sentence of the next one.

What if you need to proceed to another important topic which seemingly has no connection to what was covered in the previous paragraph?

Simple. Fabricate a transition in a logical way. For example, say you interviewed Mary Smith, the baker.

Your lead paragraph is:

Mary Smith, the baker, said she loves her job because she's allowed to sample all her goodies.

In the second paragraph, you could proceed to how she became interested in baking:

She said she has loved sweets since childhood when she used to go to Grandma's house and gorge herself on brownies.

Next, if you want to include a paragraph on what her husband thinks of her doing this job, you'll have to create a smooth transition. But, do not do the following:

She said her husband thinks she's a "certified glutton." (This isn't a smooth transition because you're leaping from her childhood to adulthood.)

For a good transition, try:

> *Aside from her lifelong love for sweets and the joy she's found in creating them, she said her husband criticizes her for being a "certified glutton."*

Journalists often use words such as "aside from," "regardless of," and "despite" to signal changes in subject matter. Use your imagination and consider other ones.

As mentioned in Chapter Two, if you're writing about a person, business, organization, etc., weave in background information toward the middle of the story, rather than waiting until the end.

Following is an exercise in putting into correct order the first few paragraphs of a jumbled story. Don't rewrite them, but cross out the wrong numbers and insert the correct ones. The correct order and explanation follow. (This is a fabricated article with fictitious facts.)

1)   Allen Porter has been making violins for 11 months since leaving R.C. Jacoby and Sons School of Violin Making in Chicago. There, he spent 3½ years learning the delicate art.

2)   Through his business, Melifluous Violins, he also repairs and restores violins and violas.

3)   Although Bunks Town may seem like an obscure place to operate this business,

Porter recognizes a need for the service in this rural northern region, and for violin instruction which Jack, his twin brother who lives with him, offers.

4)   From a farmhouse in Bunks Town, violin sounds filter from an open front window.

5)   In the living room, a violinist instructs two students. And, to the right, is a door leading to a garage in which a young, black-bearded man in overalls sits cross-legged, whittling wood. His craft is not very common—he makes violins.

6)   "I do most of the work by hand with many carving tools and gauges—these are the classic Old World methods," Porter said.

7)   "The majority of Yellow County's people used to buy or repair their instruments in Chicago, but now they don't have to travel 50 miles," Porter said. "And here, there are many people interested in learning to play violins so my brother can earn a living, too."

8)   Porter uses methods of centuries past to make and repair instruments.

Story Reconstruction

Your first paragraph should be paragraph 4. This creates a mood and encourages the reader to discover the topic.

Your second paragraph should be 5 because it introduces the story's topic of violin making.

Your third paragraph should be 1 which specifically identifies the person about whom the story is written and his business, and also weaves in his background.

Your fourth paragraph should be 2 because this further identifies the scope of Porter's business.

Your fifth paragraph should be 3 because it tells more about the business and answers the question of who the violinist is.

Your sixth paragraph should be 7 because it's a direct quote which supports the preceding paragraph.

Your seventh paragraph should be 8 because, by now, the reader is interested in methods Porter uses to do the work.

Your eighth paragraph should be 6 because it specifies methods used for the work.

Words to the Wise

Before you submit your story, have someone read it to ensure that all facts are given and clearly explained, and that you have smooth transitions between paragraphs. I never have family members read my stories, because they are usually too critical. If this is true of your family, try a friend or neighbor who is perceptive, yet encouraging.

It's also a good idea to check your spelling, especially that of proper names. People don't always spell their first and last names with the common spelling. For example, is it "Terry?" "Teri?" Or "Terri?" Is it "Smith?" Or "Smyth?" Never misspell someone's name. If you do, your credibility as a writer will be damaged in the eyes of the public, and you'll also lose credibility with editors who will ultimately hear about it.

As for spelling in general, don't expect an editor to catch a misspelled word. You'd be surprised how many editors are poor spellers. If you're not sure if you've spelled a word correctly, chances are, you've misspelled it. And, it's not uncommon for a newspaper or magazine writer to get a nasty letter from a reader, informing him to "get a dictionary." Don't think you won't get picked on because you're a freelance writer, and readers won't know where to "find" you. They'll simply write to you in care of the publication. As a matter of fact, I was once on the receiving end.

Further, editors want a close to perfect story from a freelancer. Generally, unless it's an unusual story idea, they won't even take time to return it for revision, let alone rewrite it. If it needs major work, they will usually reject the story and use one of a more experienced freelancer. Editors don't like to admit this, however.

Finally, if a story is published, sometimes interviewees will ask you to deliver copies to them. Don't do it! Instead, direct them to the publication's circulation office. You're a writer, not an errand person, and to interviewees, the article should be thanks enough for their interview time. Do not be afraid to acquire a professional, business-like demeanor. If you do, interviewees (and editors) will be prone to treating you like a pro. And, more importantly, you'll begin to feel like one.

VI

Be Your Own Editor

Have you been reading features regularly? Pick up magazines and newspapers as you're waiting in the service room lobby for your car to be repaired. What about at the dentist's office?

Many people who like to write articles, don't like to read those written by others. However, you should develop an interest in this, so your communication skills and style will develop more quickly.

Also, the more stories you read, the more analytical you'll become. And, this will help you be more critical of your own work, as you edit your own stories.

Part 1) Word Economy

One way an editor distinguishes between professional and novice writers is by their ability to economize on words when dealing with factual statements.

Extraneous words use space which is at a premium in publications. It's surprising how word thriftiness can cut an article almost in half. So, before you submit a story, make sure it's tightened.

I've devised a few word economy rules which remedy problems I find in beginners' freelance work:

1) *Omit "that," "the," and other insignificant words, when possible.*

    Example: He said that the answer is simple.

    Rewritten: He said the answer is simple.

2) *Avoid redundancy.*

    Example: He said old trucks are not expensive for him to buy.

    Rewritten: He said old trucks are not expensive for him. (Or, inexpensive)

3) *Substitute a single word for a phrase.*

    Example: The festival had its origin well before the turn of the century.

    (Note: Journalists strive to be specific. "Well before the turn of the century" is vague. Was it 1885? 1875? At least give the specific decade.)

Rewritten: The festival originated in 1875.

Another Example: He said funds are not needed at this point in time.

Rewritten: He said funds are unnecessary now.

4) *Redesign the sentence order to eliminate words.*

Example: There were nine of them in the hall.

Rewritten: Nine were in the hall.

Another Example: He said they must narrow down the number of applicants on their list.

Rewritten: He said they must narrow the applicant list.

Now, rewrite these poorly-written sentences, and be thrifty! (Answers follow).

1) A ten-day survey was taken during the period of October 5 to October 15.

2) An autopsy to determine her cause of death is scheduled to be performed next Wednesday.

3)   It will be a year before a decision is made as to whether or not to release the information.

4)   Due to the above problems, Jeff decided not to fill out an application for a scholarship.

5)   The baby was born between 7:30 p.m. and 8 p.m., yesterday evening.

6)   He was driving his car at excessive speeds up to 90 miles per hour.

7)   The death toll for July rose to five—four people just in the past week.

8)   He was a lawyer by profession, as well as an accountant.

9)   The library is located in the upstairs section of the building.

10) They were born in the town of Cannon Beach in Oregon.

11) Within a short period of time, the couple married.

12) The physical therapist designed the exercises so that the patient could strengthen all of the muscles of his body.

Answers

1)   A survey was taken from Oct. 5 to 15. (Typically, journalists abbreviate months in the same way you learned in English class. With dates, in this case, use numerals without "th" as specified by *The Associated Press Stylebook and Libel Manual,* and as quoted in full with permission in Chapter Seven.)

2)   Her autopsy will be Wednesday. (Avoid saying "next" Wednesday, since it is implied.)

3)   In a year, it will be decided whether to release information. (Journalists often prefer "whether" to "whether or not.")

4)   Therefore, Jeff decided not to apply for a scholarship.

5)   The baby was born between 7:30 and 8 p.m., yesterday. (It's best to specify the time, unless there was an unusual circumstance which prevented finding it out. In the example, since the exact time isn't specified, note that "p.m." (as in 7:30 p.m.) doesn't need specification, because one can infer "p.m." when "8 p.m." follows. Also Note: Many publications lowercase "p.m.," while others capitalize the letters. I prefer lowercasing because it saves me two less finger motions on the typewriter.)

6)   He was driving at speeds to 90 miles per hour.

7)   July's death toll was five—four in the past week.

8)   He was a lawyer and an accountant.

9)   The library is upstairs.

10)   They were born in Cannon Beach, Oregon.

11)   Afterwards, the couple married. (It's best to specify what a short period is. If this information is unavailable, write "afterwards" to shorten the sentence. As an additional note, try to avoid other unspecific words such as "soon" and "later.")

12)   The physical therapist designed the patient's exercises to strengthen all muscles.

Part 2) Story Analysis

If editing bores you, this lively story will wake you up!

"If 'Cold Calls' Freeze Brokers' Spirit, They Can Warm to the Job," by John Andrew, is reprinted by permission of *The Wall Street Journal, Copyright Dow Jones & Company, Inc., 1984. All Rights Reserved Worldwide.*

As you read it, take notes and determine whether you think it qualifies as a good feature, and whether it's written in good journalistic order. Then, number the 24 paragraphs to facilitate reading the commentary which follows.

NEW YORK—James Good is teaching a class of new stockbrokers how to use the telephone to find new clients.

"Ring, ring," says a broker, pretending he is making a "cold call" to a hot prospect, played by Mr. Good.

"Hello," Mr. Good says, in a tone that would freeze boiling oil.

"Is Mr. Good there?" the broker asks tentatively.

"No, he's not, you simpering wimp!" The class breaks into laughter.

"Is Mr. Good there?" doesn't sound authoritative, Mr. Good explains. "May I speak with Mr. Good, please" is better, he says, making it sound like a command instead of a request. The trick is to raise the pitch of your voice as you say "Good." Then drop it like a bowling ball as you say "please."

Mr. Good is an instructor with Telephone Marketing Associates, a Sandy, Utah, consulting firm founded in 1977 by his cousin, Bill Good. Telephone Marketing teaches brokers how to make cold calls—"the real Arctic-glacier cold call," says James Good, a 46-year-old former Fuller Brush man ("Fantastic training," he says) and encyclopedia salesman ("All you have to do is get in the door, and it's a done deal").

Still Hiring Brokers

Retail brokerage concerns are cutting expenses in many ways, but most, for competitive reasons, are still hiring new brokers—a lot of new brokers. Last year, Telephone Marketing gave 400 seminars, up 60% from 1982. "To the best of my knowledge, they are unique," says Lee Solot, the vice president for training at Kidder, Peabody & Co., one of several major Wall Street concerns that has paid as much as $2,500 for Telephone Marketing's one-day program. Mr. Solot finds the seminars a good investment, though he worries that some brokers may take the histrionics too literally.

"How many of you enjoy making cold calls?" Mr. Good asks his class, a group of about 70 new brokers with Dean Witter Reynolds Inc. A few hands go up.

"I see there are a couple of liars here."

Come on, admit it, Mr. Good says, you would rather "stand in a cold shower and tear up 10-dollar bills." But new brokers face an unpleasant truth: "50% of you won't be with the company a year from now, " Mr. Good says. The wrong 50% won't have developed enough clients to develop enough sales commissions to develop their continued employment.

"Is your wife a member of the D.A.R.?" Mr. Good asks. No? Maybe, he persists, you have some rich friends over at the country club? You don't have any rich friends? Well, you better learn to get comfortable making cold calls—a lot of cold calls. Mr. Good recommends that new brokers make cold calls at least seven hours a week, every week, for the first two years of their careers.

An MBA Who Flunked

"This is a business of the telephone," Mr. Good says, adding that even having a Harvard M.B.A. won't save you if you don't know how to sell. Mr. Good knew a Harvard M.B.A. once, a broker with Merrill Lynch & Co. in Beverly Hills. He wouldn't make cold calls. He doesn't work for Merrill Lynch anymore.

How do you make cold calls? Forget about the phone book. Too many pits and not enough cherries, Mr. Good says. A cherry is an interested decision-maker with at least $20,000 to invest. A decision-maker is "the guy who cuts the check."

Cold calling starts with a good list, people like dentists in New Jersey who own expensive foreign automobiles. Such lists are available for a price from list companies. There are other ways to get lists: Mr. Good doesn't recommend them, but he passes them on. He has a friend who once dated a woman at Quotron Systems Inc. to obtain a list of Newport Beach, Calif., residents who own a Quotron stock-quotation machine.

A successful cold caller also uses a prepared script. The script for the Dean Witter class starts like this: "This is Jim Good with Dean Witter, members of the New York Stock Exchange. You know who we are, don't you?"

If the prospect responds in a churlish manner, turn the other cheek, Mr. Good advises. Say "Great! Have a nice day! Thank you very much!" and hang up. Mr. Good makes it sound more like "Greathaveanicedaythankyouverymuch!" It's important, he explains, to say it fast so that you can hang up before the other guy does. That way, you establish yourself as the "rejector, not the rejectee," and you gain the strength to make more cold calls. With practice, you can say "Greathaveanicedaythankyouverymuch!" and still hit the disconnect button faster than just about anybody except doctors and lawyers.

If the prospect seems interested, it is safe to proceed with a sales pitch. At the same time, Mr. Good says, you have to "qualify for money," i.e., find out whether the prospect has that minimum $20,000 to invest. The wrong way to do this is to ask, "Are you wealthy?" The right way, according to the script, is, "If you do like the idea, would an investment of $20,000 be a problem to you at this particular time?"

If the prospect qualifies, it still is bad form to try to close a sale on the first call, Mr. Good advises. Instead, simply offer to send some informational material. After you have established a relationship with a few follow-up calls, you can try to close a sale.

After the class has finished dinner, half of them now will spend an hour on the telephone actually making cold calls. "Any of you have black-cord fever, a slight case of the chills?" Mr. Good asks. A few brokers look slightly queasy, but no one admits to nervousness.

As the brokers man phones on Dean Witter's trading floor, Mr. Good runs around the room monitoring their performance. He throws his hand in the air in disgust as he hears one man drop his minimum from $20,000 to $10,000 to $5,000. "The next thing you know, he'll be turning the guy upside down to see if he has 35 cents in his pocket to put in a passbook savings account," he says. Another broker sticks flawlessly to the script. "The man is silk," Mr. Good purrs. He scribbles "Excellent" on a scrap of paper and puts it on the man's desk.

Some brokers stick too closely to the script. A prospect expresses interest but excuses herself to go to the bathroom. "Great!!!," a broker gushes automatically. Another flubs the

line, "You know who we are, don't you?"
Instead, he asks his prospect, "You know who
you are, don't you?"

After an hour of cold calling, most of the
class has found one or two qualified prospects.
One man also has telephoned a man who
recently died—every broker's nightmare. Another was asked if he was a member of the
Republican Party. Still another fellow was
mistaken for a bill collector. A genial South-
erner from Savannah, Ga., reached a woman
who was somewhat indisposed. "I got one
couple, I think they were hunkerin' down," he
drawls. "They knocked the phone around a bit,
and then she said, 'Huh, huh, hello? Who's
this? Who's this?'"

Greathaveanicedaythankyouverymuch!

Commentary

As a feature idea, this is naturally lively, entertaining, and humorous because of the situation and
the people involved, Mr. Good and the nervous,
novice brokers. So, the story seems to write itself.

And, it isn't hard to arrange by paragraphs because the writer mainly follows the seminar's sequence and reports accordingly. The story is written in the present tense to involve the reader in the immediate action. (You may write a feature in past tense if immediacy is not essential.)

Although the story is a natural, the writer does do a superb job of observing and fact gathering, and reporting of colorful direct quotes.

The lead sentence may seem less than snappy, but then, the topic itself would attract the typical *Wall Street Journal* reader who deals with stockbrokers. Perhaps as an alternative lead, the writer could have begun the story with the ringing of a telephone as in the second paragraph.

In the third paragraph, the writer demonstrates his ability to detail what he observes. He describes Good's tone of voice as he pretends to be a client.

The writer continually capitalizes on Good's humorous personality, as in the seventh paragraph when he skillfully creates comic effect by inserting a colorful fact—that Good is a former Fuller Brush man—before a direct quote about his marketing perspectives: "All you have to do is get in the door, and it's a done deal."

(Subsequently, note that the editor inserted subheads, such as "Still Hiring Brokers," to make the long story more interesting and approachable to the reader.)

After the writer has grabbed the reader's attention with the simulated phone conversation, in the eighth paragraph, he follows with the less interesting, though important facts about the increase of brokers being hired, and he weaves in background information about Good's seminar. If the writer had begun the story with these facts, it would have read as if written in English composition form, and the article would have been ruined.

In this paragraph, the writer also uses a quote from Lee Solot, someone of authority, about the seminars. As this writer does, if you're writing about a business or service, and you want to make a statement about its effectiveness, then it's a good idea to seek an objective opinion from a client, rather than obtain a subjective one from the service provider. But, rather than paraphrase the last sentence, perhaps it might have been more effective if the writer had quoted Solot about his worries.

In the rest of the paragraphs under "Still Hiring Brokers," the writer does a marvelous job of picking out colorful quotes from Good's interaction. Good undoubtedly said more, but the writer sifts out the most interesting conversation.

In "An MBA Who Flunked," basic facts are answered about cold calling lists which the reader has probably often wondered about, and the writer also includes the unorthodox ways of obtaining lists which add to the story's liveliness.

In paragraphs 16 through 19, the writer also answers the reader's questions about the specifics of the prepared script, and to keep the reader chuckling, he deals with brokers' survival techniques and telephone etiquette.

From paragraph 21 until the end, the writer demonstrates great observation and fact gathering skills as he summarizes the most interesting details of the events after dinner. He focuses on the hilarious action: Good's monitoring of the brokers' performance (i.e., his hand gesture and scribbling on paper) and the brokers' blunders. Here, the writer's good reporting skills are at work as he circulates among brokers to inquire about interesting results.

The writer ends on a humorous note, and one can assume that the story wasn't cut by the editor. If you are writing a feature which follows the sequence of some event, it's safe to assume the editor won't chop the ending.

Part 3) Style/Journalism-English

Let's consider a variety of style points which specifically concern journalists.

For emphasis, don't underline a word, nor capitalize each letter of it. Instead, choose a word which is forceful. And, don't put quotation marks around a word unless you want to make certain the reader knows that the interviewee used that particular word.

Example: *Wally Green said he believes stamp collectors are resourceful.*

> **But:**   *Wally Green said he believes stamp*
> *collectors are "fanatics."*

A second point:

Have you ever noticed that some features are written in past tense while others are in present tense?

Consider this example:

> *Todd Davis said he loves the creativity in-*
> *volved in working with his hands. He said he*
> *prefers earning a living at making pottery, to*
> *giving art lessons as he did previously. (Note:*
> *"Davis said" is past tense.)*

Now, consider the present tense.

> *Todd Davis says he loves the creativity in-*
> *volved in working with his hands. He says he*
> *prefers earning a living at making pottery, to*
> *giving art lessons as he did previously. (Note:*
> *"Davis says" is present tense.)*

Whichever tense you feel comfortable using is fine, but don't be inconsistent and switch from "Davis said" to "Davis says" in your story, as I find that beginning writers often do.

As for other style points, journalists have their own "language" which sometimes differs from English. The Associated Press, a wire service which supplies news organizations with stories from throughout the U.S. and the world, composes a style manual so journalists can have a reference point on term usage and abbreviations, for example.

Style manuals, such as *The Associated Press Stylebook and Libel Manual,* are textbook length, and frankly, many staff journalists don't regularly take time to refer to the abundance of rules. And, many publications create their own style which deviates somewhat from this manual.

I think, therefore, that it's unnecessary for beginning freelancers to learn an abundance of style manual details, but there are common ones which many editors follow, which you can, too. (When you become a seasoned freelancer, it will be worth your while to refer to the Associated Press manual.)

I've synthesized what I've found to be the most commonly-used rules by beginning freelancers. If you adhere to these Associated Press rules, editors will consider your work to be neat and professional. Sometimes, there appears to be no rhyme or reason to Journalism-English, but remember that certain abbreviations save space and are practical to use in journalistic publications.

From The Associated Press Stylebook and Libel Manual. Reprinted by permission of Addison-Wesley Publishing Co., Inc., Reading, Massachusetts.

1) *Dates*: Always use Arabic figures, without *st, nd, rd* or *th*.

2) *Times*: Use figures except for *noon* and *midnight*. Use a colon to separate hours from minutes: *11 a.m., 1 p.m., 3:30 p.m.*

   Avoid such redundancies as *10 a.m. this morning, 10 p.m. tonight or 10 p.m. Monday night.*

(Note: The Associated Press specifies time and day of week, in that order. When mentioning an event which will occur more than a week away, many editors follow a time, (complete) date, place sequence.

Example: The festival will be at 2 p.m. Monday, Feb. 1, 1999, at Grover City Hall.

Important: Be sure to include the weekday, so you don't inconvenience the reader who will have to look it up.)

3) *Last*: The word *last* is not necessary to convey the notion of most recent when the name of a month or day is used:

Preferred: *It happened Wednesday. It happened in April.* Correct, but redundant: *It happened last Wednesday.*

But: *It happened last week. It happened last month.*

(Added Note: From The Associated Press style, it's evident that days of the week are not abbreviated in sentences, as I've seen many students mistakenly do.)

4) *Ages*: Always use figures. When the context does not require *years* or *years old,* the figure is presumed to be years.

Ages expressed as adjectives before a noun or as substitutes for a noun use hyphens.

Examples: *A 5-year-old boy,* but *the boy is 5 years old. The boy, 7, has a sister, 10. The woman, 26, has a daughter 2 months old. The law is 8 years old. The race is for 3-year olds. The woman is in her 30s* (no apostrophe).

5) *Dollars*: Always lowercase. Use figures and the *$* sign in all except casual references or amounts without a figure: *The book cost $4. Dad, please give me a dollar. Dollars are flowing overseas.*

For specified amounts, the word takes a singular verb: *He said $500,000 is what they want.*

For amounts of more than $1 million, use the *$* and numerals up to two decimal places. Do not link the numerals and the word by a hyphen: *He is worth $4.35 million. He is worth exactly $4,351,242. He proposed a $300 billion budget.*

The form for amounts less than $1 million: *$4, $25, $500, $1,000, $650,000.*

(Pay particular attention to the fact that according to Associated Press rules, a round dollar figure is not followed by a decimal with two zeroes.)

6) *Cents*: Spell out the word cents and lowercase, using numerals for amounts less than a dollar: *5 cents, 12 cents.* Use the *$* sign and decimal system for larger amounts: *$1.01, $2.50.*

7) *Dimensions*: Use figures and spell out *inches, feet, yards,* etc., to indicate depth, height, length and width. Hyphenate adjectival forms before nouns.
   Examples: *He is 5 feet 6 inches tall, the 5-foot-6-inch man, the 5-foot man, the basketball team signed a 7-footer.*
   The car is 17 feet long, 6 feet wide and 5 feet high. The rug is 9 feet by 12 feet, the 9-by-12 rug.
   The storm left 5 inches of snow.

Additional Style Suggestion

Sometimes, though not often, I've found that my feature students use numerals in the context of fractions, percentages, and speeds. For more details on numeral usage, consult *The Associated Press Stylebook and Libel Manual.*

Part 4) Story Analysis

Let's take a break from mechanics and analyze a story with beautiful style. Following are the first seven paragraphs of "Slow Descent into Hell," by Jon D. Hull, a magazine story about the homeless, published in *Time*. Here, the writer goes to live on the streets of Philadelphia in winter to report first-hand about conditions of the homeless. The story is superior for the writer's observation, description, and fact gathering. Comments follow each paragraph.

This is the first paragraph:

A smooth bar of soap, wrapped neatly in a white handkerchief and tucked safely in the breast pocket of a faded leather jacket, is all that keeps George from losing himself to the streets. When he wakes each morning from his makeshift bed of newspapers in the subway tunnels of Philadelphia, he heads for the rest room of a nearby bus station or McDonald's and begins an elaborate ritual of washing off the dirt and smells of homelessness: first the hands and forearms, then the face and neck and finally the fingernails and teeth. Twice a week he takes off his worn Converse high tops and socks and washes his feet in the sink, ignoring the cold stares of well-dressed commuters.

Paragraph 1—This is a great lead paragraph. First, the lead sentence haunts you: "A smooth bar of soap...is all that keeps George from losing himself to the streets." The reporter identifies George only by his first name to protect identity and family privacy. This is sometimes done when covering features of a personal nature, including those about the retarded or mentally ill. Also, first name only lends to the anonymity of a homeless person whom the public often perceives as a nobody. Further, note how the writer makes the reader feel as if he's present and watching by describing "a makeshift bed of newspapers." To amplify vivid effect, he is specific about the restaurant rest room of a "McDonald's" and "Converse high tops." And, the writer observes how George washes himself, and in the last sentence, he astutely observes how others react to George and how he copes with them.

This is the second paragraph:

George, 28, is a stocky, round-faced former high school basketball star who once made a living as a construction worker. But after he lost his job just over a year ago, his wife kicked him out of the house. For a few weeks he lived on the couches of friends, but the friendships soon wore thin. Since then he has been on the street, starting from scratch and looking for a job. "I got to get my life back," George says after rinsing his face for the fourth time. He begins brushing his teeth with his forefinger. "If I don't stay clean," he mutters, "the world ain't even going to look me in the face. I just couldn't take that."

Paragraph 2—George's background is woven in. By now, you're curious about how he became homeless. Also, the writer grabs you with a good direct quote early in the story with George's slang—"I got to get my life back...the world ain't..." The writer's good observation is further revealed as he describes how George brushes his teeth.

This is the third paragraph:

George lives in a world where time is meaningless and it's possible to go months without being touched by anyone but a thug. Lack of sleep, food or conversation breeds confusion and depression. He feels himself slipping but struggles to remember what he once had and to figure out how to get it back. He rarely drinks alcohol and keeps his light brown corduroy pants and red-checked shirt meticulously clean. Underneath, he wears two other shirts to fight off the cold, and he sleeps with his large hands buried deep within his coat pockets amid old sandwiches and doughnuts from the soup kitchens and garbage cans.

Paragraph 3—Observation flourishes with meticulous description of specifically how George dresses. And, the writer creates pathos by revealing how George combats cold, and how and from where he hoards food. We also learn that George isn't a drunk, an important fact which we wonder about.

This is the fourth paragraph:

Last fall he held a job for six weeks at a pizza joint, making $3.65 an hour kneading dough and clearing tables. Before work, he would take off two of his three shirts and hide them in an alley. It pleases him that no one knew he was homeless. Says George: "Sure I could have spent that money on some good drink or food, but you gotta suffer to save. You gotta have money to get out of here and I gotta get out of here." Some days he was scolded for eating too much of the food. He often worked without sleep, and with no alarm clock to wake him from the subways or abandoned tenements, he missed several days and was finally fired. He observes, "Can't get no job without a home, and you can't get a home without a job. They take one and you lose both."

Paragraph 4—The writer creates more pathos by describing George's efforts to find work and leave the streets, dispelling some people's myth that all homeless people don't want to work. He also reveals universal problems of the homeless, such as their trying to find work without having a home, and holding a job while lacking what many take for granted.

This is the fifth paragraph:

George had $64 tucked in his pocket on the evening he was beaten senseless in an alley near the Continental Trailways station. "Those damn chumps," he says, gritting his teeth, "took every goddam penny. I'm gonna kill 'em." Violence is a constant threat to the homeless. It's only a matter of time before newcomers are beaten, robbed or raped. The young prey on the old, the big on the small, and groups attack lonely individuals in the back alleys and subway tunnels. After it's over, there is no one to tell about the pain, nothing to do but walk away.

Paragraph 5—The writer continues with George's plight and universal problems of the homeless. He also continues with good direct quotes using George's slang. He is adept at understanding George's emotions and problems of the homeless, especially as revealed in the last sentence, "...there is no one to tell about the pain..."

This is the sixth paragraph:

Behind a dumpster sits a man who calls himself Red enjoying the last drops of a bottle of wine called Wild Irish Rose. It's 1 a.m., and the thermometer hovers around 20 degrees, with a biting wind. His nickname comes from a golden retriever his family once had back in Memphis, and a sparkle comes to his eyes as he recalls examples of the dog's loyalty. One day he plans to get another dog, and says, "I'm getting to the point where I can't talk to people. They're always telling me to do something or get out of their way. But a dog is different."

Paragraph 6—From the back alleys and subway tunnels of paragraph 5, this new paragraph begins with a smooth transition (behind a dumpster) about another homeless man. This new "character," a drunk, is one whom many may consider to be a typical homeless person. Here, the writer's fact gathering is thorough: how cold it is (an important fact), and details about Red's background, including his name's origin. The writer demonstrates heart-warming observation, "...a sparkle comes to his eyes as he recalls examples of the dog's loyalty." The writer also keys into Red's alienation from others and his perception of how others scoff at him for his drunkenness.

This is the seventh paragraph:

At 35, he looks 50, and his gaunt face carries discolored scars from the falls and fights of three years on the streets. An upper incisor is missing, and his lower teeth jut outward against his lower lip, giving the impression that he can't close his mouth. His baggy pants are about five inches too long and when he walks, their frayed ends drag on the ground. "You know something?" he asks, holding up the bottle. "I wasn't stuck to this stuff until the cold got to me. Now I'll freeze without it. I could go to Florida or someplace, but I know this town and I know who the creeps are. Besides, it's not too bad in the summer."

Paragraph 7—The observation is haunting. There's subjectivity: "At 35, he looks 50..." There's pathos with the picturesque observation: discolored scars, teeth jutting and missing, and baggy pants and frayed ends. The writer relays a good direct quote and even vividly describes that Red said it while holding up a bottle.

Important Lesson: As this writer illustrates, you can write a beautiful story if you make use of your senses when you gather facts or go out to interview someone. In so doing, you'll allow the reader to fully experience the situation.

VII

Finishing Touches

Part 1) Page Format

Let's touch on a few technicalities. For neat and professional-looking copy, you can use the following simple page format for your submission. Also, it's best to triple-space your stories so editors have room for notations. Further, always indent for a new paragraph, rather than use the block style.

First Page (Illustration Follows Directions)

1) *Upper left corner:*

    A)   Name
    B)   Address
    C)   Day/Eve. Phone
    D)   Social Security Number (For Payment)

2)   *Halfway down the page*

A)   On this page only, begin halfway down the page to give the editor room to make notations for the typesetter. Center the "head" (also called "headline"). This means the article's title. Keep the head short. The editor will probably change it due to space limitations. But, try to make the head snappy to lure the editor.

B)   Directly beneath the head, write your "byline" (i.e., By John Doe).

C)   Skip a few lines and start your story. For newspaper stories, you can use a "dateline" as a professional touch. This means the name of the city or town where the interview took place. However, newspaper feature editors usually omit the dateline if the story originated in the same town where the newspaper is based. Example: If you submitted a story to a San Francisco newspaper and the interview took place there, a dateline is unnecessary. But if the interview took place in nearby Sunnyvale, then include the dateline (followed by a dash) before you begin the story. (Don't bother with datelines on magazine stories.)

Usually, when submitting an article to a newspaper in another state, you should include in the dateline the name of the state where the story originated, after the town's name. Example: If you interviewed someone in Elmira, New York and submitted the story to a Montana newspaper, your dateline would obviously be unclear without mention of New York.

Journalists abbreviate most states in datelines. When they do, their abbreviations are sometimes different than those used by the U.S. Postal Service. For abbreviations of states and comprehensive dateline details, you could consult *The Associated Press Stylebook and Libel Manual.*

3)   *At center bottom:*

The word "continued" should be placed here to signal more pages.

Name
Address
Day/Eve. Phone
Social Security Number

"Head"
By John Doe

SUNNYVALE—Story starts — — — — — —
— —
— —
Start new paragraph — — — — — — — —
— —
continued

Second Page

1) *Upper left corner:* Place words "Add 1" followed
by a dash. "Add 1" means "one page added to
first page." Following the dash, write the "slug."
The slug is the first few words (about three)
taken from the head to identify the story.

Should your story pages become separated, the editor can readily find them by the slug and place them in order.

2) Skip about two lines and continue your story from the first page.

3) *At center bottom:* Write the word "continued."

Third Page

1) Upper left corner: Write "Add 2" followed by a dash. Following the dash, write the slug.

2) Skip about two lines and continue the story from "Add 1" page.

3) *At center bottom:* Write the word "continued."

Fourth Page

1) *Upper left corner:* Write "Add 3" followed by a dash. Following the dash, write the slug.

2) Skip about two lines and continue the story from "Add 2" page.

3) *At center bottom:* If this is the last page, write "-30-" which means "The End." If this isn't the

last page, write "continued" and go on to "Add
4" page, etc.

4)   If this is the last page, your "copy" (article) is
now neat!

5)   Staple your pages together.

Part 2) Story Analysis

Next, let's continue the chapter with a light
feature.

"Can-Do Classic in Midwestern Town," by Andrew H. Malcolm, reprinted from *The New York
Times,* is the kind of feature idea which you can find
throughout the U.S. It's the type which Charles
Kuralt, network television newsman, finds in his
cross-country travels.

Pay attention to the qualities which make it a
good feature. After reading it, number the paragraphs to readily follow the commentary.

ELLISVILLE, Ill.—For 59 of her 60 years
Helen Myers has loved books. First, her mother would read to her. Then the little girl began
paging through books herself. Finally she

began reading them, aloud at first and then silently.

In fact, Mrs. Myers loves books so much that she founded a library, the Ellisville Public Library, which struggles to survive here like a lonely wildflower in a crowded cornfield.

The library has one room and a dedicated staff of one: Mrs. Myers. For the last 22 years Mrs. Myers has regularly trooped the four blocks from her house down to Main Street in this prairie community hard by the Spoon River. There sits her laboriously collected array of old and less-old volumes, more than 2,000 of them lined up on handmade shelves and in old cardboard cartons just waiting in case one of the struggling town's residents is moved to read.

Earning a living is a physical activity in these rural communities. So sitting around, even reading, is not a trait that has earned widespread admiration over the years. Officially, Mrs. Myers's library is open one day a week, every Saturday morning from 9 until 11. "I look forward to Saturdays so much," says the librarian, "I just love being around books."

Unofficially, everyone knows the librarian's home phone number where a call at almost any hour will bring Mrs. Myers running to lend one more book. Some weeks she may have as many as five customers. "That would be a real good crowd," she says.

•   •   •

But running a library singlehandedly in a crumbling Midwestern community is not easy these days when mere economic survival is a victory. For one thing, there are fewer people living here, what with the simultaneous declines in area farming, mining and manufacturing. Ellisville used to have 400 potential readers; now there are 140, actually 135 since the Mahr family just left.

There is more competition for free time, namely television. "It's much harder for kids to read now," she says. "It's so much easier just to push a button and let the TV do their thinking. It's true. If you read, you tend to do your own thinking. I try to tell parents—carefully, you know—they ought to limit their kids' TV. But they use it as a babysitter. That's the way the world's going."

To this day she recalls the wonder when her mother took the time to read to her out loud and the exhilaration the little girl felt while racing through the pages of *Call of the Wild*, which took her to wondrous places so far from home. "Oh, *Call of the Wild* was wonderful," she recalls, "I've read it four times so far."

So, to help increase library patronage she has suspended the penny-a-day penalty for late returns. She has come up with a new idea: a reading hour for children. "Maybe," she says, "I can get a few hooked on books."

She's put signs in the library window and at
the Post Office. And when no one comes by
for the reading hour, Mrs. Myers tries to
round up a few listeners with some phone
calls. "I know I'm competing with the Saturday
cartoon shows," she says, "but I'm going to
read old standards like *Black Beauty* and, oh,
of course, *Treasure Island*. Just like my mother.
I figure if in all these years I get just one
person to read a book, my time's not wasted."

•   •   •

Mrs. Myers recently finished cataloguing all
her books, most of them donated and old. And
she's already taken care of the roof problem.
It took five years of cajoling, fund-raising and
begging, but this fall she finally had $350 in a
savings account, enough to buy lumber and
shingles to rebuild the tiny library's rotting
roof. Steve Morris, Kenneth Effland, her
husband, Ken, and Keith Sullivan, who is 83,
donated their labor up on the roof.

The Skelly gas station manager provides
free butane to keep the library warm most of
the time. A woman in California sends $10 a
month to help with the electric bill. And the
librarian finances any other expenses out of
her Social Security check.

But Mrs. Myers's can-do spirit now seems
to be infecting other townsfolk. In the last two
years various groups combined to raise $500
for playground equipment. They had a three-

day 150th birthday party for the town this year, even though someone counted wrong and it was really the 151st birthday. They got a special governor's citation for civic spirit.

And now comes the prospect of a small baseball diamond for Ellisville's remaining children. An owner of two small lots has offered to sell them for $200 apiece, not an inconsequential sum for real estate transactions here. Mrs. Myers is holding out for $150 apiece.

"I tell you," says Mrs. Myers, who hasn't figured out yet where the funds will come from, "We've got some kind of big plans around here."

Commentary

This story is not merely one of an individual and her efforts to found a small-town library, but the larger theme is about a town and its community spirit. If you had discovered this story idea, you may have started the interview thinking that it would be just about Helen Myers and her library, but as the interview evolved, you would have caught on to the larger theme and worked it into the story.

The lead paragraph draws you into the story through its nostalgia about childhood. The reader recalls his own childhood when reading about Myers.

In the second paragraph, you learn the story's topic through the marvelous simile, "...Library, which struggles to survive here like a lonely wildflower in a crowded cornfield." It emphasizes the rurality and the odds against the library's survival. (Note: Courtesy titles, such as "Mrs.," are used in the more formal publications such as *The New York Times*.)

The third paragraph emphasizes the small-town ambiance, with the short commute from home to Main Street, and the fact that it's an economically-depressed area. It also specifies the "make-do" library with no new books, handmade shelves, and cardboard cartons.

Fairly early in the story, in the fourth paragraph, there's a direct quote from Myers about her love for the library and books. This would have lost some of its meaning had it been paraphrased.

The fifth paragraph reinforces the small-town flavor—calls to the librarian's home and on-call hours.

Following, the story is divided into parts by dots which the editor most likely arranged.

The story's second part focuses on the fact that although the town is rural and perhaps backward due to its economic depression, modern attitudes, such as television being popular over reading, prevail. The small-town flavor is accentuated and personalized with the recounting of the Mahr family's relocation, and thereby a decrease in population...and library readers.

In the seventh paragraph, today's widespread attitudes about reading vs. television is woven into the story through a good direct quote from Myers. And, this is aptly contrasted (with a smooth transition in the next paragraph) with the old days of Myers' childhood and her excitement about books. Thus, you recognize her dedication to increasing the popularity of reading with today's children through reading hours.

The second part ends with quotes in paragraph 10 which emphasize Myers' humanitarian spirit in helping others: "...if...I get just one person to read a book, my time's not wasted."

The story's third part focuses on civic spirit with the library's financing. The writer personalizes this small-town story as he names specific individuals as helpers with the community project. Here, you especially view Myers as the quiet hero in these last few paragraphs, as she has motivated others in civic spirit and positive thinking, despite the town's poor economic state.

In the last paragraph, Myers' determined personality shines through. If the writer had instead paraphrased this paragraph and omitted "I tell you...," the reader would have lost the flavor of Myers' determination. However, here, as throughout the story, the writer is adept at nuance.

The only thing the story lacks is a physical description of Myers.

A Final Word

Go out and find a story idea like this one. Charles Kuralt-type of stories are naturals. With some practice and concentration, you can conduct a good interview and write a good story, just as this writer did. And, people enjoy reading small-town civic spirit stories in today's modern society, out of nostalgia for simpler times. Of course, these stories are also popular with editors.

VIII

Getting Published

IMPORTANT: IN THIS CHAPTER, I INCLUDE DISCUSSION OF PAYMENT FOR ARTICLES. OF COURSE, I SPEAK IN BROAD TERMS, AND YOU WILL FIND EXCEPTIONS TO MY ESTIMATIONS. YOU SHOULD ALSO REALIZE THAT EDITORS OF PUBLICATIONS OFTEN DON'T CONSIDER INFLATION WHEN PAYING FREELANCERS FROM YEAR TO YEAR. FREELANCE PAYMENT AT MANY PUBLICATIONS CAN BE STATIONARY FOR EVEN FIVE YEARS, ESPECIALLY AT THE SMALL ONES, SO IT'S BEST TO CULTIVATE YOUR SKILLS SO YOU CAN MOVE AHEAD TO THE LARGER ONES.

You've written your story, but you're not through. Now, you must market it. If you're unpublished or have had one article published, start "small." This means locally, with community or neighborhood papers, or suburban editions and supplements of the nearest metropolitan paper. In so doing, you'll build credibility and experience so you can advance to larger, more prestigious publications. It's better to start "stringing" (freelancing) for local newspapers than for local magazines. With the former, you're published quickly (within a few weeks), rather than waiting months as with magazines. As a beginner, you need these immediate rewards for self-confidence and motivation.

At community or neighborhood papers, you may approach the top dog, that is, the editor or managing editor. Personal contact counts with editors. It's like job hunting—you don't just fling a resume, but attempt to pay a visit. At community papers, the editor will introduce you to the feature editor (sometimes called "living," "lifestyle," "people," "family" editor, etc.) Or, you can directly approach this editor. Note, however, that sometimes there is no feature editor at community papers, but the paper's editor oversees features. (There is no feature editor at neighborhood papers, either.)

Phone the community paper for the lifestyle editor's name. (Note: On the newspaper's Opinion/Editorial page, it lists the editor and top officials, but it doesn't list department editors such as the feature one. Also, if you see the title "Editor and Publisher," don't be confused. This means "publisher," and don't approach him unless the publication is so small that there isn't an editor.)

If there is a lifestyle editor at a small paper, he either has little or no budget for freelance features. So, you may have to surrender your first story for free or for as little as $25. First, ask if pay is offered. If it isn't, decide whether you'll give away the story or whether you'll try a publication which prefers published writers and pays well. Community papers have some regular "correspondents" (freelancers) who are paid nominally for news and features, but if you're not a regular writer for them, the editor may not pay you.

As for visiting an editor, do so at 2 p.m. when he's usually in, but not busy with morning deadlines or meetings. Don't phone ahead for an appointment, because if he doesn't know you, he'll likely say he doesn't need any freelance stories. Instead, drop in and let him glance through your story so he'll become interested. Take two or three minutes of his time to inform him of the story's topic and why the story is good. (Before the visit, you may phone ahead only to verify if the editor is in, but hang up as the receptionist transfers your call. And, in case the editor steps out sometime after you've made the call and before you've arrived at his office, it's a good idea to have prepared a note which you can attach to your story which says you dropped in and left the story, and that you'll be calling later in the afternoon to confirm he got it.)

Whether you actually speak to the editor in person or catch him on the phone after you've dropped off the story, don't be intimidated if he's abrupt, because journalists are always hurried. Tell him you'd like your byline on the story if he publishes it. The majority of editors do give them, but you may meet an exception who leaves the story's freelance writer unidentified.

Allow the editor two days to read your story. Then call to ask if he's read it and plans to run it. If he says he hasn't read it, then check again in another two days. Until the editor definitely says he won't run it, keep after him.

What if you're not aggressive, you say? Then assume that posture when dealing with editors! Getting published is about 65 percent tenacity and 35 percent writing ability.

Community papers are a good start because their editorial staffs are informal and have about 10 people, and you won't be barred from newsrooms. You can easily develop contacts and graduate to being a columnist or staffer there, if desired. (By the way, staffers at community papers are poorly paid and work long hours, but these positions are considered very good training ground for reporters.)

Remember, in submitting a story to a publication, your topic must be connected to the area which the publication circulates in, to interest its audience. For example, if you wrote a feature about a person living in Town X—instead of Town Y in which the publication circulates—there would have to be some relationship to Town Y, such as if the article is about the person's business which is located in the latter town.

Also, remember that seasonal stories, particularly holiday ones, must be submitted well in advance of the celebration. In general, with newspapers, this could be as early as a month in advance. And, with magazines, this might be as much a six months in advance. You'll have to check with the particular publication.

If your first story is published without pay, next, progress to a paying publication. The joy of getting published will probably soon wear thin if you continue to receive no pay or little pay for your efforts. If there is a metropolitan area nearby, its metropolitan paper usually has zoned editions which cover suburbs. Or, if the metropolitan paper is located in another region of your state, it probably has a zoned edition which includes your area. Each zoned edition has an editor who runs news and features from your area. Writing for zoned editions is like writing for a small paper within a metropolitan paper. The editors (sometimes called bureau chiefs) can be approached as you would those of a small paper, because bureaus are personalized with a dozen or so reporters. Call the bureau and ask for the chief's name. It's best if you can visit to leave your story and also include photocopies of articles you may have previously gotten published which the editor can peruse. With a zoned edition, you would generally get $50 or more for a feature.

As for other sections of the metropolitan paper, there are special consumer supplements, such as food ones, which are either published weekly or during holidays. The pay range is broad, and they accept inexperienced writers with an interest in that topic. If you like to write about food, for example, approach the food supplement editor, perhaps with a story about an ethnic restaurant. This article would include facts about the business and its owner, such as how long the owner has had it, what he likes about being in the restaurant business, what kind of clientele the restaurant caters to, what the owner's goals are for the business, etc. (Note: If you include these kinds of facts, the article won't sound like a restaurant review. But, of course, you should also mention what kinds of dishes are served, and you can include the owner's favorite recipe.)

There are also advertising supplements, such as real estate ones, which call for articles on how to purchase a home, for example. You could interview home inspectors for an article of this kind.

After you've built some credibility with stories published by suburban or regional bureaus, or supplements of a metropolitan paper, you've attained some exposure and prestige.

Next, graduate to the metropolitan paper's feature section which circulates in every edition, because this allows greater exposure. It pays well, usually $100 or more. Approach the feature editor, because at metropolitan papers, there's an editor for each section of the paper. (Don't contact the managing editor or editor, because at metropolitan papers, they are policy people who don't even know the hundreds of editorial staffers.)

Besides the feature section, try the metropolitan paper's travel section, a relatively high paying section, offering a few hundred dollars or more. It's usually 99 percent freelanced. Approach the travel editor.

At a metropolitan paper, the highest step for a feature freelancer, considering pay and prestige, is its Sunday magazine supplement. This may pay $1000 for a cover story. Here, the exposure is greatest because the paper's Sunday circulation is higher than that of weekdays. But, don't approach the Sunday magazine editor until you've built up a feature portfolio from the other newspaper sections. (However, these editors often run autobiographical essays of non-published writers, if you like to do this type of writing.)

The Sunday magazine is heavily-freelanced and usually runs local and regional feature topics. With heavily-freelanced publications, the editor usually offers writer's guidelines, upon request. These reveal the publication's objective and target audience, what material it seeks and what it doesn't want, along with facts about manuscript length, pay, etc.

After you've been published locally, you may want to try regional papers and their Sunday magazines. For example, if you live in Southern California, you might try a Northern California paper. Your county library usually has the major regional and national papers in its newspaper room (Sunday editions), including their back issues of a month or so. Go there and browse the feature section or Sunday magazine to see what freelance features are run. Besides the byline mentioning "Correspondent," a freelance story can often be identified as such, if the byline is followed by "for" plus the publication's name. If it's not freelanced, the byline is followed by "of" plus the publication's name, or the story is identified as a submission from a news, syndicated, or wire service, such as Associated Press (AP) or United Press International (UPI). Beware, however, that in a few cases "correspondent" can mean a "staffer." For example, publications (and television networks) which have bureaus nationwide, have correspondents (staffers) at their smaller offices. But, journalistic organizations without these nationwide bureaus, usually call their freelancers "correspondents."

With regional papers, you don't always have to call long distance to find out the names of specific editors, but can often find them in *Editor and Publisher International Yearbook*, a library reference book. It lists U.S. daily and weekly papers, first alphabetically by state and then by city, including addresses and names of their major editors. It also includes Canadian and foreign papers and news and syndicate services. Say you have an artist-friend in Oshkosh, Wisconsin about whom you want to write. Check the Yearbook's weekly and daily newspaper sections to determine which publications are based there.

Your county library usually has on microfilm the major metropolitan newspaper of your state (going back decades), or back issues of the hometown community paper, along with various community papers in your state. Also browse these papers' living sections of the past few months and see what kinds are features are published. It's better to target a publication you want to write for, and then locate a story idea, than vice versa, because if you write a great story which isn't suited to any publication you know of, what use is it?

As for mailing stories out of your area, it's often difficult to get them published because you lack personal contact with editors. The stories might not even be read unless you have a contact there, it's costly to call long distance to follow up, and it may take months before you receive a response about whether it will run. Also, if the publication is slow in responding, you may need to write after a few months to inquire about the story's status. (If I don't get a response after a few months, I proceed to submit my story elsewhere, because unusually long waits are often fruitless.)

However, you can have much success if you mail to small publications or those which aren't nationally prestigious, but which offer good exposure and pay. A publication with 10,000 circulation or less, for example, is small, while one with 100,000 or more is large. *Gale Directory of Publications* and *Writer's Market*, library reference books, include circulation figures of individual publications. Often, the larger the circulation, the more the publication pays and the harder it is to be published. Incidentally, editors calculate that the actual number of people being exposed to a publication is actually four times the circulation figure. So, for example, a circulation of 10,000 actually means that 40,000 people are reading it.

Writer's Market, updated annually, includes listings of a few thousand publications which buy freelance stories. (These entries are only a fraction of the enormous U.S. market, because practically any publication will consider freelance material, if submitted.) But among its listings are hundreds of small and mid-size magazines offering excellent pay—sometimes equal to that of the prestigious national publications commonly found in U.S. homes and on newsstands—and they are relatively easy to be published in. For example, smaller magazines, such as trade or company ones, may pay hundreds of dollars for features. And, when you read their stories, you'll say, "I could have written something better!"

Writer's Market is arranged by subject, such as men's, women's, travel, and religious publications. Each entry details what kinds of articles the publication runs, what percentage of the publication is freelanced, article length and pay, and whether writer's guideline sheets can be requested. Although the library's current edition is a reference one, the library often circulates prior editions. Don't, however, get one that's more than a year old, since markets change rapidly.

Writer's Digest monthly magazine, also at your library, includes detailed information on numerous new and existing publications which accept feature articles. And besides, it has timely articles on writing and selling all kinds of mediums (fiction, poetry, etc.) In general, it's a good source for giving writers confidence and courage to keep up their momentum.

As for writer's guideline sheets, they sometimes state that queries are required before submitting manuscripts. If so, editors want specifics on your story idea to decide whether they're interested, instead of wading through an article. Write a one-page query describing the topic and who you'll interview. It should be lively to spark interest, indicating why you've chosen the topic, how it's perfect for the particular publication's needs, and specifically how you'll craft the story to excite its audience.

If you have the choice of sending a query or the entire manuscript, I'd choose the latter to give the editor the best idea of what you have to offer. With the mailed manuscript, include about a four-sentence cover note explaining the story's topic, who you are and what you do for a living, and where you've been previously published (if applicable). On the cover note, list name, address, day/evening phone numbers, and social security number for payment, as well as on the manuscript's first page. If you have been previously published, also enclose a copy of one or two of your better "clips" (articles clipped from publications) as confirmation. Incidentally, always keep a photocopy of your submission because editors often lose or misplace them, and be sure to enclose a self-addressed stamped envelope for return of your manuscript, in case it's not published.

When guidelines state that stories are sometimes assigned, realize that this primarily involves writers whom the publication has previously published. If you've had a few features published by a publication, you can reveal your interest in assignments. And, as a regular freelancer, you'd be in a great position to negotiate for better pay!

At publications, editors often change. Six months from now, you may be dealing with a new editor who has changed the section's focus. So, if you want to regularly write for it, keep reading to notice changes.

Magazines, in general, are harder to get published in than newspapers, simply because they appear less often, so they usually run fewer freelance stories. A story submitted to a newspaper may take from two weeks to two months to be published (except for Sunday magazines which tend to publish them after several months). Typically, newspapers don't pay until the story's been published. To get published in magazines, it may take six months to a year. When it takes that long, magazines usually pay upon story acceptance. However, if the writer's guidelines sheet states that the publication won't pay until the story runs several months later, it's probably wise to submit elsewhere. Besides the aggravation of waiting for payment, it's possible that in the interim, another editor will take over and cancel your story.

If your story is rejected, don't discard it, but consider your writing efforts, and submit it to a second choice. Rejections can occur for several reasons, which may not have anything to do with whether or not the story was well-written. Maybe, for example, it was rejected because the editor ran a story on a similar topic shortly before, or perhaps the editor has a personal bias toward the topic.

If your story is rejected a second time, keep trying! (I base my number one submission choice on which publication pays the most and work downward to the least paying one. You may have different priorities, such as which publication you most enjoy.)

If your story is published, don't be surprised if an editor changes wording and distorts a fact, deletes important sentences, rearranges the paragraph order and makes it confusing to read, etc. Editors aren't always careful, and some are just bad. If you don't like an editor, stop writing for him. As a staffer, you'd be stuck with him, but as a freelancer you aren't.

Remember, it's very difficult even for established writers to get published in top national publications. These publications may pay $1000 or more for a story. Despite your good writing record, you may need a contact there to get results, and former staff writers are sometimes favored. Consider prestigious publications after many years of writing.

Once you've gotten excited about writing, you'll want to browse unique bookstores or tobacco shops in your town for publications from other states which aren't at supermarkets. Of course, you'll find it's costly to buy many publications for your own reference library. Alternatives are: determine whether a publication offers a free sample or one for a nominal charge through, for example, *Writer's Market;* check whether there's a publication exchange at your library with decent variety; and purchase magazines' back issues at a used bookstore for as little as a quarter, though not those older than a year due to possible format changes. (Sometimes magazine issues, a few months old, circulate at the county library.)

Photography for Features

An important part of a feature is its supporting photography. With submissions to a local publication, you usually don't need to obtain photos, because the editor will dispatch a staff photographer if he decides to run the story. However, if you mail a story out of the area, and it's accepted, you'll need to submit photos. But, don't worry if you don't take photos, since there are easy ways to obtain them from competent photographers. For example, call the photography department at a local publication for names of area freelance photographers, or staffers who freelance in their spare time. Or, if you submit a travel feature from a vacation spot, the local chamber of commerce might provide free photos, if you inform it of your intent.

In its writer's guidelines, you may often find that a publication wants you to state photo availability with your submission, in case it's accepted. If so, state that you'll provide the publication's preference. (The guidelines include preferred photography specifications.)

If possible, avoid the inconvenience of sending photography until you've been notified that your story has been accepted. Also, consider that photography could get misplaced by the editor if he hasn't specifically asked for it.

Sometimes, however, a publication requires that you simultaneously submit your manuscript and photography for consideration. Of course, if you don't do your own photography, you can't very well ask a photographer to do the work if there's a chance your story will be rejected. In this case, it would be best to select a publication without this requirement.

If your story has been accepted, before you send a photographer out, it might be helpful to have him/her read your story to obtain photo ideas pertaining to the subject. Also, photographers welcome writers' input about possible photo ideas which would support the story.

When you submit photos, include the photographer's identification notes about the "who, what, when, wheres" for "cutline" (caption) use. When the photos are received, the publication will pay the photographer.

In reading publications' guidelines, are you surprised that you may double your money on a submission if you do the photography? Yes, photography can pay as much as a story, because a publication pays based on space which the work occupies, and not on the amount of job time spent. As a writer, I say photographers have it easier!

Rights

As for publication rights, it's best not to sell all story rights unless you're paid a large sum. When all rights are sold, the publication won't pay you more for a reprint in another one of its editions, and you can't sell the story in its present form elsewhere, nor include it in a future book. If the publication wants all rights and offers little money...negotiate! If the publication is far away, respond immediately by certified mail so your letter doesn't get to the bottom of the editor's stack. Ask if he'll either pay you more money for all rights (state a price based on what their pay range is, or what you think is fair considering the publication's circulation size), or whether he'd be willing to settle for first rights only for the pay he originally quoted. This works, so don't be bashful!

It's better to sell stories for first rights only, so you can sometimes resell them. Usually, if you sell a story to a local general interest publication for first rights only, you can probably find a specialty or trade publication, or even a general interest publication in another region which would buy your article as a reprint. You can get more mileage money-wise and exposure-wise this way. If you resell, just be sure the publication is clear on where and when it was previously sold.

In general, always be clear on what rights you are selling to a publication. If you mail off a submission to a publication and you do not know what rights it normally buys, inquire in the cover note.

And, if you end up making an alternative arrangement for rights than what is normally offered by the publication, it's good to have a written record of this special arrangement. Drop the editor a note confirming the alternative agreement you made with him, and keep a copy for your files.

When you become a seasoned freelancer, you might want to consult *Writer's Market* for a comprehensive discussion of rights.

Added Note: Never show an editor, as some beginning writers do, how thrilled you are that he's decided to publish your story. Play it cool, especially if you plan to write for his publication again. If you don't, the editor may get the idea that you write primarily for the joy of getting published, and aren't very concerned about money. I've met too many freelancers who don't care about writing for money, and this is probably the major reason why freelance writing is not a high paying field.

Expenses

Concerning your writing activity, keep an expense record, such as for interview miles traveled or gas money spent, paper, typewriter ribbon, photocopies of an article, dictionaries, file folders, this book, etc. You may be able to claim tax deductions for them, so get into the habit of being miserly and not overlooking any related expenses.

Story Logs

When your story is published, log its head in a notebook for quick reference, along with a one-sentence description of what it's about, and where and when it was published. (It's also handy to write the date the story ran directly on the clip. And, so you don't accumulate a pile of clips in a manila folder which could easily get torn, paste each clip to a sheet of paper. Using this method, it also makes it easier to sift through the folder when looking for a particular clip.)

Consider These Publications

As for specific publications, how about considering local professional magazines? Are you a lawyer, banker, or teacher? Write features for the local bar, banking, or educational association publications.

Do you have a hobby such as stamp collecting? Write for a stamp collector's publication.

Are you a college or graduate student? Consider your school newspaper.

Do you spend time at the beach or mountains? Write about a person or amusement there, and submit it to a publication in that area, or to a travel magazine.

Generally, these types of publications invite inexperienced writers, have national exposure, and pay up to several hundreds of dollars:

1) Airline magazines—They run many general interest features from different regions—people, places, sports, events.

2) Alumni magazines—Consider not only those of your schools, but also ones which accept features from non-alumni who write about interesting alumni.

3) Americana magazines—They like features on craftspeople, places, events, sports, foods from all regions.

4)   Business magazines—Consider particularly those which run features on entrepreneurial ventures or unusual small businesses.

5)   City magazines—Target particularly those published by chambers of commerce. They appreciate features on innovative businesses and a variety of profiles on movers and shakers.

6)   Company or corporation magazines—Many run general interest features through their house organs, especially those published by the utilities. Submit features on people, travel, food, crafts.

7)   Craft or interior decorating magazines—The latter particularly pay well. Both like how-to stories.

8)   Ethnic and minority publications—They appreciate features about successful people in business, arts, politics.

9)   Hobby or recreational magazines—Those that pay well usually focus on expensive hobbies, such as boating.

10) Music magazines—They pay well for features about nationally-famous musicians, or up-and-

coming ones from different regions of the country.

11) National association or club magazines—They like profile features about humanitarian members.

12) Political magazines—Those that pay well represent republican or democratic concerns, rather than the smaller parties. Try features on up-and-coming politicians from your area.

13) Regional magazines—Also consider those which aren't Sunday newspaper supplements, such as those published by associations or electric cooperatives. The latter particularly like regional lifestyle features.

14) Religious publications—Some pay surprisingly well, and they like features about people and social services.

15) Senior citizen magazines—Senior newspapers usually don't pay well, but magazines do. The latter like features on interesting seniors, travel, health information (staying fit), social services.

16) Trade magazines—They like features on movers and shakers and advancements in the field.

17) Travel magazines—Consider particularly those of automobile clubs or oil companies. Besides travel stories, they run how-to stories on hobbies and recreational activities.

The Last Word

Now that you've read this book, don't let much time lapse before you begin searching for a story idea and writing. Now, the information is most fresh in your mind, and your enthusiasm is at a peak!

You're on your way to being a published writer!

Appendix

Library Treasures

For Story Ideas:

* Newspapers/Magazines—local, regional, and national.

* At your public library, check Adult Services Department or information tables for brochures, newsletters, and pamphlets about local organizations, community services, activities, etc.

* *On The Road with Charles Kuralt*,
  By Charles Kuralt, G.P. Putnam's Sons, New York, 1985.

  This book is good to read because it illustrates how easy it is to come up with feature story ideas. A word of caution: Ignore the style Kuralt writes in, because he's a broadcast journalist and is not writing in print journalism style.

Basic References For Getting Published:

- *Writer's Market,* Writer's Digest Books, Cincinnati, Current Edition.

  Includes thousands of listings for magazines and newspapers which accept freelance material. Gives details on what kinds of material publications seek.

- *Editor and Publisher International Yearbook,* Editor and Publisher Co., New York, Current Edition.

  Includes listings of daily and weekly newspapers in the U.S. with names of major editors at these publications and circulation size.

- *Gale Directory of Publications,* Gale Research, Inc., Detroit, Current Edition.

  Includes listings of newspapers and magazines in the U.S. and their circulation size.

Writing Resources
(For more advanced feature writing skills and style):

- *Writer's Digest* magazine, F & W Publications, Inc., Cincinnati.

  Monthly magazine which includes helpful articles for freelancers on feature writing. Also includes updated information on publications to sell material to.

- *Writing Creative Nonfiction,* By Theodore Cheney, Writer's Digest Books, Cincinnati, 1987.

  Author focuses on style for advanced writers.

- *Basic Magazine Writing,* By Barbara Kevles, Writer's Digest Books, Cincinnati, 1986.

  This book is a misnomer because it's too advanced for beginners. It includes information on how to write and get published in prestigious magazines and negotiate for "big bucks."

- *The Art and Craft of Feature Writing,* By William E. Blundell, New American Library, New York, 1988.

- *The Associated Press Stylebook and Libel Manual,* Editor: Christopher W. French, Addison-Wesley Publishing Company, Inc., Reading, Mass., Fifth Printing, September 1988.

Index

Order Form

Please send me _____ copies of *Beginners' Guide to Writing & Selling Quality Features. A Simple Course in Freelancing for Newspapers/Magazines.*

I enclose $12.95 for each copy, plus $1.50 for shipping per book.

Name _____ Phone _____

Address _____

City/State/Zip _____

My check, payable to Civetta Press, in the amount of $ _____ is enclosed. Mail to Civetta Press, P.O. Box 1043, Portland, Oregon 97207-1043, U.S.A. Phone: (503) 228-6649.

QUANTITY ORDERS INVITED

This book is available at special quantity discounts for bulk purchases. For details, contact Marcia Ray or Maria Marotta, Marketing Department, Civetta Press.

SAN: 200-3171